How to Make People
LISTEN
(without being *pushy*)

For Win
With much
gratitude.
Keep listening!
Jean

99 Coaching Tips
for Powerful
Conversation

JEAN HUDSON

Printed in Canada

ISBN: 978-0-9867970-0-2

First Edition

Cover Design by Sue Impey

Book and cover layout by By Design Desktop Publishing Inc.

Published by execuCoach International Corporation

Library and Archives Canada Cataloguing in Publication

Hudson, Jean, 1949-

How to make people listen (without being pushy) : 99 coaching tips

for powerful conversation / Jean Hudson.

Includes index.

ISBN 978-0-9867970-0-2

1. Oral communication. 2. Conversation. 3. Listening. I. Title.

P95.H83 2011   ·   302.2'242

C2011-901568-4

FSC

Mixed Sources
Product group from well-managed
forests, controlled sources and
recycled wood or fiber

Cert no. SW-COC-003773
www.fsc.org
© 1996 Forest Stewardship Council

Dedication

For my beloved David.

Acknowledgments

I want to thank the students, teachers, coaches, clients, colleagues, family and friends who have encouraged and supported my work over the years. Without you none of this would have been worthwhile or anywhere near as much fun. Your names are carved on my heart.

WHAT OTHERS ARE SAYING ABOUT THIS BOOK

"**How to Make People Listen** is immediately applicable to anyone wanting to grow their circle of influence. I felt as though Jean was there, guiding me through each interaction. A copy should be in every car and on every desk for those wishing to communicate effectively! This book is the closest we can come to a travel size version of Jean and her expertise!

Kurtis Frederick, Real Estate Investor, REB Canada

"Jean is a no nonsense coach who exudes her love for people and her desire to see them succeed in every breath she takes and every line she writes. She offers these 99 tips as 'an invitation to Success' for the reader and that is exactly what she delivers. Well written, well presented and in a format that allows readers to get maximum benefit!"

Monica Santiago, owner, On Page Productions

"A must read for anyone who talks or listens! I learned a great deal about what I am doing, what I can do, and best of all, I have gained a guide and reference that I can refer to again and again to refine my communication skills."

L M Wannetta Johnson-Hamrell, Calgary Bookkeeping Etc.

"Clear and concise, sometimes humorous, and packs a powerful punch! Jean Hudson has condensed an enormous amount of great advice into a very practical, readable book of coaching tips and exercises that are already changing the way I listen and speak. Cultivating awareness in a conversation today helped me turn a sceptic into a client."

Linda Orr Easthouse, Founder East House Natural Health Centre, Health Kinesiology Instructor

"*The cry of every human heart is to be heard.* When you get this, really get it, you get Jean Hudson. She encourages you to communicate so your heart can be heard, and listen so everyone else's heart can be heard by you. Every tip in this book is to move you to this authentic place and gives a resounding Yes! as the answer to this question: *I can hear you, can you hear me?*"

Terry L. Hansen,
Author Genius by Choice for College Students

"Jean Hudson has provided a wealth of information, physical, strategic and mental, to help all of us communicate better. Having had issues in this area myself for many years and with many audiences, it is wonderful to find a resource that deals with it all. After reading this invaluable book, and practising, you too can master the art. A must read for the professional or the amateur keen on stepping up their game."

Chris Hylton, MA, Calgary

I am not a teacher;

only a fellow traveler

of whom you asked the way.

I pointed ahead – ahead

of myself as well as you.

– George Bernard Shaw

CONTENTS

INTRODUCTION

We don't pop out of the womb with conversation skills. Babies don't know what to say or how to say it – when they are uncomfortable or in pain they yell until someone listens and gives them what they want. (Some adults are still squawking when they are forty.)

Most of us were socialized early to believe that in order to be fed and cared for we needed to ask politely, wait our turn, stand in line, and wait for someone else to give us permission to speak. Some of us learned that children are to be seen and not heard, and many of us, myself included, unconsciously carried all those rules into adulthood.

As adults, even though we have the freedom to say and do whatever we want, and to be as powerful as we wish, we may not be comfortable doing so.

However, if we are extraordinarily lucky and avid learners, as I am, we eventually learn that we have the right to express ourselves, to be heard, to change and grow in our own unique ways. And if we meet people who listen to us and love us as we are, we may even feel safe enough to give voice to our deepest thoughts.

I believe that each of us holds wisdom gleaned from a lifetime's experience gained the hard way – by learning how to avoid pain and achieve what we want. From as far back as I can remember, I hated being *second* – second born, second best, second in the class, and *just a girl*. Never the first to be heard or consulted.

I yearned for *listening*. I wanted to be allowed to express myself. I wanted my voice to be heard and understood.

Given that start in life, it is no wonder that I've spent so many years studying how people use language – how they express themselves, and how they get others to listen. Of course, I've put my foot in my mouth repeatedly, but somehow that hasn't stopped me. I am still fascinated by how communication impacts the quality of our lives. And I am so far from understanding it all that I'll need to live another sixty years to maybe get it *right*.

Yet I do know one thing for sure: Language reveals us to ourselves and to others. It is a beautiful gift we can use to share ourselves and our ideas with others. Knowing that is what has driven me to write, and to keep learning further ways to fully express who I am and what matters to me.

The tips here have been absorbed from the mentors, teachers, writers, clients, children, and friends who have willingly shared their wisdom and knowledge with me. I've experimented with the strategies and adapted them for my work, just as I hope you will. Although I don't know exactly how they will benefit you, I know they've helped hundreds of others to voice their ideas and be heard.

And I know I would enthusiastically recommend them to the people I care about most in the world.

Now I share 99 strategies here for you, with my love and hope that they will somehow strengthen your conversations and ease your journey.

Jean

PS: My writing style, like my coaching style, is casual, frank, and forthright. It may be a bit blunt for some readers. I trust that you will recognize that my intent is to encourage and challenge you to see conversation differently, and to express yourself with integrity and power.

"The truth ain't the truth until they believe you;

and they can't believe you

if they don't know what you are saying;

and they can't know what you are saying

if they don't listen to you;

and they won't listen to you

if you aren't interesting;

and you won't be interesting unless

you say things freshly, originally, and imaginatively."

Bill Bernbach (1911-1982)

IMAGINE

How much discomfort have you suffered, how many opportunities have you missed, because someone wouldn't listen to you? How many nights have you lain awake wondering what you could have done or said differently? How much hair have you pulled out over an otherwise great employee, colleague, prospect or even a family member who can't/won't/doesn't listen?

You have ideas, knowledge, and value to contribute. You have experiences, strategies and suggestions that could help people solve problems and reach their goals – if only those people would actually listen!

Imagine for a moment that you could wave a magic wand and clients, contacts, and decision makers – even your own family – would listen attentively to what you have to say. What would that look like? Sound like? Feel like? What would happen to your life and your business? In what ways would that listening be good for you – and for them?

Well, this book isn't a magic wand, so waving it around won't help. However, the strategies you now have in your hands can work like magic in business or personal conversations. Whether you are interacting one-to-one, attending a meeting, or addressing a roomful of strangers, these tips can help you be more powerful and effective.

What would be possible in your life and work if you knew you could make people listen whenever you wanted?

Perhaps you would feel more confident and relaxed when meeting new people, or more at ease in your family. Perhaps you would tackle a dream you've been postponing, or make a greater contribution to others' well-being. Perhaps you'd like to strengthen and deepen your business or personal relationships. Or maybe you'd love to increase your income by turning business prospects into loyal clients and raving fans.

It's been my privilege over the years to hear success stories just like those from people who have worked with the contents of this book. The best part of it all is that virtually anyone can use the strategies to ensure their voices are heard and understood.

It doesn't matter where you start reading and applying the tips; it only matters that you *do start*.

COACH TO COACH...
(Yes, you're a 'coach', too.)

Whether you call yourself a coach, a consultant, a strategist, a sales manager, an educator, a financial planner, a team player, a leader, an entrepreneur, an executive, an employee, a partner, a friend, or a parent – *you are a coach* if you need to be able to:

- tap into the best of yourself or others, and
- cause effective action to be taken.

Coaching happens every minute of the day, in all walks of life and in every situation. Each of us coaches in many different ways throughout the day.

Our success as coaches depends on our ability to assess needs, handle difficult issues, influence, inform, encourage, inspire, and challenge ourselves and others to take think clearly and take focused action.

This book was written specifically for you, the coach, and the people you will help. Although you can't actually *make* anyone listen, you can learn how to draw others in to what you are saying, and influence them move into action – action that will take them to where they want to go and beyond. But first they need to hear you. Your messages need to penetrate.

The tips contain proven techniques that have helped me, and thousands of others, to:

- pay focused attention in conversation without losing sight of their goals
- communicate ideas effectively in business and personal situations
- conversationally influence the results they want.

You have valuable ideas that other people could benefit from – if only they would listen! Unfortunately, others cannot learn what you know if you don't express yourself in ways they can hear and process. Therefore it is always your responsibility to attract, and hold, the ears and eyes of the people who need what you have to share.

As you read this book, remember that each tip is an invitation to success, not a rule to be obeyed. Apply them one by one, or in various combinations. I encourage you to be flexible in how you take advantage of them to create results you want, and trust you will adjust the strategies to suit your specific circumstances, taking into account the

- timing and purpose of the conversation,
- relationship dynamics,
- specific environment, and
- communication styles and interpersonal skills of everyone involved.

To make the most of this book, you need only a healthy curiosity and a willingness to try out new approaches. You'll get to play with the ideas, experiment with different tips, and use the strategies to help you express yourself in ways that people can't resist.

So relax, breathe, and keep reading. You're going to make an even greater difference, *Coach*.

WHY PEOPLE DON'T LISTEN AND WHY IT'S SO HARD TO GET THEM TO!

It's no one's fault that some people (maybe even you) don't listen well sometimes. Although good listening skills rate high in studies of leadership and relationship effectiveness, such skills are exceedingly rare. Why? Because:

- Only a tiny percentage of people have ever had any formal listening training. They don't know *how* to listen, or *what* to listen for.

- Real listening requires deliberate conscious attention and focus. It does not happen automatically.

- Human beings have become accustomed to, and in some cases addicted to, high levels of noise, stimulation, and action. Listening, however, isn't an adrenalin rush.

- People get caught up in their own thoughts and agendas, losing track of what is happening for those around them.

And, for as many individual reasons as there are individuals.

Why Joe doesn't listen

Joe's clock radio blasts him awake at 6:00 am and blares while he showers and dresses. As his coffee brews, he hastily pours a bowl of cereal and slurps it down while half-watching the morning's bleak television news: crime, conflict, and a foul weather forecast. His stock portfolio lost several points again, and his favorite football team was trounced last night. He's already in a bad mood, and the day has barely begun.

Joe checks the clock. Yikes, 6:35, he's going to be late! He throws his bowl into the sink with a clatter, races up the stairs for business papers he left by his bedside the night before, and stuffs them into his briefcase. He pulls the pillow off his wife's face, tells her it's time to get up for work, kisses her on the cheek, and races downstairs and out the door. He doesn't hear his daughter calling "Daddy..?" as the door slams behind him.

He reverses the car over his son's bike helmet in the driveway, launching it into the neighbour's hedge. Swearing aloud, he doesn't stop. He turns up the radio to take his mind off everything there is to do today: the project he didn't finish yesterday, his declining consulting income, impending deadlines, staff issues, and the argument he had with his wife last night. It doesn't work. His mind won't stop racing – not now, not ever.

He mentally reviews his *get-it-done-yesterday* list of tasks for the day, and rehearses his one-minute introduction for the breakfast networking meeting. In the back of his mind, the issues in his marriage cry for his attention, but are forced into submission by his worry about what the people at the meeting will think about his ideas. He honks ferociously at any driver who cuts in front of him on the freeway, and his fists and jaw clench in frustration when he is forced to slow to a crawl past construction crews.

By the time Joe arrives at his breakfast meeting he is over-stimulated, preoccupied, and unfocussed – a fairly *normal* state of mind for him.

An hour later, Joe leaves the meeting with a pocket full of business cards. He doesn't remember connecting well with anyone, and isn't sure if he will follow up with the cards he collected. He thinks the whole event was a waste of time because he didn't get a chance to say everything he wanted to say, and no one there said, *Yes, I need your services.*

What Joe doesn't realize is that his new acquaintances and prospective associates won't bother to follow up with him, either. They felt ignored, frustrated by Joe's focus on his own wants and needs, and by his inability to pay attention to others who were talking. (Joe's wife and kids feel the same way.) No one at the meeting gave him that feedback, though. If they had, Joe would be surprised. He *wants* to listen, he *thinks* he is listening. But he isn't.

Why Joe Needs You to Make Him Listen

So how do you handle a prospect, client, colleague, or relative like Joe? He probably won't enroll in an effective listening course just because you want him to pay attention to what you are saying. In fact, he would likely resent your suggesting it – he thinks he *is* listening!

But Joe doesn't know what he doesn't know. He's like most of us. Many intelligent, successful people don't know how to listen, or to speak effectively about themselves and their business so others will listen. And it isn't easy for any of us to acknowledge that:

- *we* are responsible for the results we are getting,
- criticizing others or ourselves for poor communication skills is a waste of time and energy, and that
- effective communication requires conscious attention to both listening and speaking.

While you can't change Joe, you can change the approach you take with him. You can grow quickly in the ability to ensure your message is heard and understood. And though you can't *make* Joe listen by force or coercion, you can certainly *influence* him! Even small shifts in your approach can lead to significant changes in Joe's response.

Just because Joe isn't in the habit of listening doesn't mean he can't or won't listen. It means that when you are talking to Joe you must develop a relationship quickly, establish good reasons for him to listen, and engage him fully in the conversation. That's *your* job. Then Joe will listen. And he may even be grateful you made it easy for him.

THE MASTER KEY TO POWERFUL CONVERSATION

You're it! *You* are the master key. Only you have the power to control your world – your conversations, your thoughts and behaviours, your life, your business. If you want people to listen to you, then it's up to you to make sure that happens.

Who you are and how you think about yourself and others directly impacts how effectively you get your message across.

The first key to any change is to know yourself and what you want to achieve. When your purpose is clear to you, and you are comfortable within yourself, that comfortableness will be transmitted in how you express yourself. And as you control your approach in accordance with your desired outcomes, you will be able to direct your verbal and non-verbal communication to create exactly the results you want.

Does that sound impossible? It is, if you try to tackle everything at once. Fortunately, even small changes can make a significant difference in results.

Who are you and what are you thinking?

The crucial first step is to become aware of what you are thinking, doing and saying. Treat this as research. To conduct the research, you *catch yourself* in the act of communicating. You become aware of exactly what you are thinking, saying, and doing moment by moment. The objective is to be able to see and hear yourself as others see and hear you.

Pay conscious attention to both your speaking style and your internal attitudes. Be honest with yourself. Some of what you are doing is already working well for you, but some is not. Even your current frame of mind influences what you say and how you say it. What is working for you? What isn't?

No matter what you discover, please maintain a willingness to face the truth without blaming yourself or others. Remember that each of us is doing the best we can with what we have learned so far, and as long as we are breathing, there is more to learn.

What do you want?

Why do you want people to listen to you? Be certain that your purpose for being in any conversation is clear to you. Know what you want to accomplish and prepare your approach, as well as your mental and emotional states of mind, to achieve it.

How do you want people to respond to you? Do you want them to laugh, cry, calm down, empathize, reveal themselves, refer you, get angry, take action, decide quickly, make a specific change, embrace your cause, partner with you, understand you, elect you, agree with you, hire you, follow your directions, or...? What do you want them to think, feel, or do in response to you?

Knowing the response you want will help you focus what you say and how you say it so people *get it*.

What I want is for you to benefit from the tips here. Read, use and reuse this book. Study it, highlight it, write notes in the margins, doodle in the blank places – whatever makes the words come alive for you. Then get out there and test the strategies. Pay attention to the results you get with various people. Celebrate your victories and learn from any mistakes. Keep experimenting until they listen.

"Courage does not always roar.... Sometimes it is the quiet voice at the end of the day, saying, 'I will try again tomorrow.'" Anonymous

Your next successes are up to you.

Acceptance

Powerful conversations thrive when we accept people and situations exactly as they are. No one is going to change how they listen simply because you want them to, so there's no point advising, ordering, suggesting or otherwise trying to make them listen your way. It won't work. What you say and how you say it can greatly *influence* situations, and may spark change, but the actual choice to change or not belongs to each individual.

You do not have to like or approve of what people are saying, or how they respond to you. That's their business. Your task is to deal with reality – *what is* rather than *what you would like it to be.* Acceptance of reality can be difficult because it requires that you stop trying to change anyone or anything other than yourself, but the results are worth the effort.

When people know you genuinely accept them as they are, they tend to open up to you and hear what you have to say. Meeting them where they are at makes it so much easier for you to take them where you want them to go.

Please grant yourself acceptance too. You'll make mistakes and encounter difficulties, just like the rest of us growing, learning human beings. Take it easy on yourself.

Related tips: Respect, Judgment, People matter

Accountability

No matter what others are feeling, thinking, or expressing, *you* are the one in control of everything you think, say, and do. You are accountable for your words, your tone, your feelings, and your responses. You are responsible for whether or not what you say is worth being listened to – interesting, engaging, relevant, and clear. Making communication work for you is never the other person's responsibility.

Reflect honestly. Are you blaming other people or circumstances for your behaviour or attitude? That will sap your power. Instead, take full responsibility for managing your own attitude and actions in conversation. What the other person says is about him, not about you. Everything *you* say or do, however, is about you. Ensure that what you say reflects who you are and what matters to you.

Maturity requires that you hold yourself accountable for the results you create, without blaming or shaming anyone.

Related tips: Judgment, Showing up, Boundaries, Attitude

Agreement

Don't start talking without checking if the prospective listener is prepared to listen. A person could be in the middle of an important document or conversation when you phone, or deep in thought when you approach them. If you start blasting your ideas into their space, it won't exactly endear them to you or your message. Take care to set the stage for good listening by ensuring that you have the other person's willing attention.

When you initiate a phone call or conversation, ask if the person has time to talk (about your subject). Let them know exactly how long it will take, and ask for their time and consideration.

As well, keep the agreements you make about conversations. Start and end them on time, and keep them on topic. If you say you only need five minutes to explain idea A, don't speak for twenty minutes about ideas A to H.

A word of advice about advice: If you don't have permission to give advice to someone, and it isn't part of your job responsibility, resist the temptation. Unsolicited advice is always unwelcome. Even if you are an expert in your industry, be sure to ask the person if she would be open to some feedback. Get a clear agreement, or keep your advice to yourself.

Related tips: Manners, Timing, Interest, People matter

Articulation

When you clearly articulate your words and sentences and pronounce them clearly, you make it easier for others to listen to you. Understanding will be compromised if you mumble or if your accent differs greatly from the listener's. (Outside our own culture, we all have *accents*.)

To articulate more clearly, deliberately slow your speech, ensure your lips are visible, and pronounce each word clearly. Do not *swallow* the last syllable of words and sentences, as often happens with English speakers.

One of my Asian friends speaks English distinctly when he focuses on enunciating the words. When he forgets, I can barely understand a word he says. Fortunately, we are used to each other, so when I say "Whoa!" we laugh, and he repeats what he had said. However, most people won't tell you that they didn't understand. Later, when they don't remember what they said, you may wonder why they didn't *listen*.

Why should you bother to pay conscious attention to your articulation? Because it will make it easier for others to understand you and respect your ideas. Isn't that what you want?

PS: Articulation is also important when you are speaking by phone, as there are no visual clues to help the listener understand what you are saying.

Related tips: Clarity, Voice quality, Audience signals

Assertiveness

What you have to say matters just as much as what others have to say. It is your responsibility to remember that and to speak your truth with courage and firm confidence.

While confrontation is not usually appropriate (although sometimes it is necessary to clear the air), being upfront and direct are always preferable to indirect hinting about what you mean or what you need. Speak up. Don't expect anyone to read your mind or guess what you mean. They'll get it wrong 100% of the time.

Be open, honest and direct. You do not need to protect anyone's feelings, nor do you need to trample on them. Simply speak kindly what is true in your experience, claiming your own opinions. Those who lay their cards on the table rather than holding them close to their chests are seen as refreshing. They are welcomed.

Be willing to ask your listeners for what you want, so they know *how* you want them to listen. If you want them to help you solve a problem, they'll need a different listening approach (critical thinking and prioritizing) than if you simply want them to hear you out (patience and compassion).

Related tips: Confidence, Interrupting, Courage

Attitude

Your attitude impacts what you say and how you are heard. No one wants to listen to surly, disgruntled, angry, frowning creatures. Ask yourself what attitude you are bringing to your conversations. If you don't much like your frame of mind, neither will anyone else. If your manner is condescending, arrogant, unreceptive, docile, fearful or dismissive, people won't know how to be comfortable in your presence, let alone listen to what you have to contribute.

Of all the attitudes you could bring to a conversation, none is as important as genuine curiosity. Do everything you can to remain curious about people, possibilities, and processes. Curiosity sparks creativity, and breeds genuine interest in others – a rare quality that will draw people to you and to your message.

As Einstein said, "The important thing is not to stop questioning. Curiosity has its own reason for existing. One cannot help but be in awe when he contemplates the mysteries of eternity, of life, of the marvelous structure of reality. It is enough if one tries merely to comprehend a little of this mystery every day. Never lose a holy curiosity."

Related tips: Enthusiasm, Tone, Fresh eyes and ears

Audience signals

Watch your audience (1 or 100) as you speak. When you have captured their attention and imagination, they will let you know.

Typically, engaged listening shows as stillness, body and eyes turned to speaker, open posture, eye contact, relaxed body, alert eyes and a face that changes expression in response to the speaker's words. Some listeners will respond to your message with laughter, groans, responses, nods, head tilting or other gestures to show they are paying attention.

When you notice a person or a group has lessened listening signals, or dropped eye contact, look directly at them, pause in the middle of a sentence, and wait. When you have eye contact again, ask a question that leads in to what you want to say next. People cannot resist questions. They will re-engage.

Sometimes a non-responsive listener is thinking deeply about what you have said, is confused or disinterested. Blushing may indicate an uncomfortable topic, and slightly pursed lips or raised lower eyelids could indicate disagreement or thoughtfulness. (If people are fleeing from you, you are probably too intense.)

You do not need to consciously know what every person's signals are, but it is important to notice when changes occur. You may even choose to interrupt yourself and ask if the listener has concerns or questions.

PS: If for any reason you suspect you are losing your listeners, it's safe to assume that you are correct. Change your approach to regain their attention.

Related tips: Awareness, Observation, Non-verbal cues

Authenticity

Dare to be authentic. There is no need to over- or underplay your abilities and experience. Tell the truth as you see it, kindly and openly. Give people the gift of the real you – as is, without pretense. The real you (even if it's the fallible, vulnerable side of you) is always more charismatic and convincing than any persona could be.

You might choose to adjust your demeanour and language for better effect, but don't try to be someone you are not. A naturally quiet and calm human being who is trying too hard to be assertive and expressive is painful to watch. Be true to yourself. People respect genuineness.

Related tips: Flexibility, Vulnerability, Connection

Awareness

If you could only read one tip in this book, this is it! Awareness is the key that ensures all the other tips in this book, and that all aspects of personal and professional growth, work well.

In conversation, awareness is the human capacity to step back and observe oneself in the act of speaking and listening – to be conscious of sense data, behaviour and patterns. Basically, you *catch yourself* doing whatever you are doing. Awareness allows you to observe yourself with a discerning but non-critical eye.

When you are aware and alert, you allow yourself to see and hear a conversation as it is, rather than as what you think it should/could/might be.

As you become more aware of what you are thinking, what you are doing, what you are saying and how you are saying it, you create opportunities to choose which behaviours to keep and which ones to let go. But until you are aware of what you are doing, you cannot recognize what you need to change in order to reach your goals. (That's because, just like the rest of us, you don't know what you don't know until you know it.)

Conscious awareness brings new information to your attention. Then you can decide what actions are needed.

Related tips: Showing up, Observation, Judgment

Being memorable

In the small business world that I play in, getting noticed and remembered is critical for success. You have to stick out from the crowd if you want to be remembered. When business building, networking and socializing, there is little room for ordinary. You must be distinguishable from your competitors.

Calm firm strength is called for, and just enough outrageousness to impact other people's memories. The human brain notices and remembers what is novel, different, or emotion-laden. So dare to be novel and different. It's quite fun, anyway!

People will always be interested in what you have to say if you contribute useful comments while being interesting, memorable and lively. You don't just want to be listened to in the moment – you want to be remembered later, when others need you or your services.

When I don't want to be seen as a coach among coaches (sometimes there are several at an event) I call myself a Professional Listener. People have told me months later that they can't hear the word *listening* without thinking of me. I like that they remember.

An acquaintance I haven't seen in years wears scrubs and uses this line every time he introduces himself: "Computer sick? Call Doctor Vic!" Even though my son is in the same field and always fixes my computers, Vic still pops into my mind each time a computer is *sick*. That's memorable.

What can you say to make your name, your service, or your products memorable?

Related tips: Audience signals, Enthusiasm, Impressions, Energy

Beliefs

What you believe about yourself, others, and the communication process affects what you say and how you say it. All beliefs are limiting. They keep you from doing what is not in alignment with your values. That's a good thing, if it means you speak and behave kindly, honestly and with integrity. However, not all beliefs support effective conversation.

If you believe that the only way to get what you want is by force, you will be too intense to create engaged listening. If you blame others for your effectiveness in conversation, you will continue to be ineffective. If you believe people won't listen no matter what you say or do, you will prove yourself right. (We love to prove ourselves right.) If you believe that you are too shy or introverted, you will be – even though many shy and introverted people have no trouble getting people to listen.

If you believe that what you have to say is just as important as what others have to say, you will speak up and be heard. If you consider that everyone has something of value to offer, you will create an open listening space for others and yourself.

What beliefs move you forward, and which are you allowing to limit you?

Related tips: Assertiveness, Authenticity, Courage

Boundaries

You are responsible for teaching people how to treat you. You don't have to listen to anyone, and no one has to listen to you. Each person has the right to define their own limits and criteria for satisfaction – how, when, where, with whom, and about what topics they will communicate.

Be clear about your own boundaries, and please respect the boundaries of others. It's mature and responsible to say "No" to any inappropriate time, place, or topic.

If you allow others to breach your boundaries, the cost could be your time, energy, emotional or physical well being – and their respect for you. Your caring for others is admirable, but not at the cost of taking care of your own needs and preferences. Speak up.

For example, if someone starts complaining at length, he's not likely to stop and invite you to share your more constructive ideas. So speak up quickly and stop the complaining before it gets out of hand.

A simple statement that you would rather talk about lighter topics can work, but if the complainer really wants to continue, and disregards your request, there's little value to be gained in listening to him. He is not going to listen to you. If you don't want to waste your time or ruin your mood, politely get out of the conversation quickly.

For a friend or client in crisis (assuming she isn't in crisis every week), ask how you can best help. If what she wants is for you to hear her out, and you have the time available, then listen. If she wants advice, help, or a change in attitude, it's up to her to ask for it. Keep to a time limit that you are comfortable with.

Related tip: Time, Assertiveness, Exit strategies, Agreement

Breathing

Regularly take a few deep breaths when you are not speaking, and listen to the air moving in and out of your lungs. This will bring your attention into the present, and clear your mind so you can fully show up for the conversation, and stay focused on the goals you wish to achieve.

People unconsciously notice and match others' breathing patterns. Try this out: Next time you are listening, match the speaker's breathing pattern, noticeable in the slight rise and fall of the chest. Breathe as shallowly or deeply, as quickly or slowly as he is. How do you feel – more tense or more relaxed?

When people are listening to you, they will match your breathing pattern. If you speak breathlessly or tensely, you will unknowingly make your listeners nervous and tense, as they are not getting enough air!

Slow your breathing to a nice easy pace, and breathe deeply. Your listeners will relax along with you. Focus on allowing your words to flow as you exhale, and inhale easy breaths at natural pauses – where there would be commas, or periods in written work. This is actually a very natural process.

For practice, watch videos of effective speakers, and follow their breathing patterns.

Related tips: Pace, Pitch and Projection, Voice quality, Rapport

Brevity

People listen in sound bites. They don't know how to sift through a flood of words to find your main idea, so don't launch a lot of ideas into the conversation and expect others to figure out which ones you wanted them to focus on. Deliver your message in clear concise sentences, and keep it brief.

If you expect that others can or should follow your long stories or explanations, you will be disappointed. Get directly to your main points quickly, while you have everyone's focus. If they want more information they will ask, or... if what you say is interesting, they will keep listening to hear the details.

Once you have established a reputation for being a person who gets your message across quickly, you will attract people eager to engage in conversation with you.

Related tips: Clarity, Counting, Structure

Clarity

Plan your main points ahead, and stay focused on your key messages. Say only what needs to be said. When people think out loud, pause often, or fail to get to the point, they lose control of the conversation, and invite the listeners' minds to wander. (Sometimes the listeners' bodies wander right off, too.)

It's hard for others to listen and understand if you do not speak clearly. Speak plainly and simply, with enough volume to assure listeners that you are in control of yourself and your message. This builds trust as well as respect. Do not mutter or mumble. Do not cover your mouth, or have your mouth in any way disguised (by an unruly beard, for example). Subtle lip movements are often picked up as communication assistors. Anything that detracts from others' ability to make sense of what you are saying will lessen your ability to get your message through.

If for any reason the listener is not able to clearly understand what you are saying, they will shift their attention to the environment, the lint on your shoulder, or their own thoughts. Listening will end there.

Related tips: Articulation, Language, What you say, Brevity

Commonality

People want to know that you are just like them in some way. You can be more persuasive on any subject if you find out what you have in common with your listener first, and make a strong connection on a personal level before delving into business matters.

Hobbies, sports, vacations, family, and your experiences of life, when they overlap with the listener's, help build a personal bond. I've heard accounts of new acquaintances finding a common interest in golf over dinner, playing nine holes the next morning, and inking a deal in the afternoon. A small business owner is more likely to hire the bookkeeper mom she met at her daughters' soccer practice than she is to hire one from the Yellow pages.

Since we humans are more alike than we are different, it is always possible to find something in common with each person you meet.

Related tips: Connection, Being memorable, Stories matter

Confidence

We are magnetically attracted to people who have confidence in themselves, their skills, their plans, and their messages.

Confidence on the outside comes from an internal knowing that you can handle whatever happens. It can only be gained from accomplishment. You can't get it by studying, planning, or thinking about it. You can only get it by actually experiencing success.

Others are not as confident as they may seem to you. Each of us has areas of lesser experience and skill. And confidence is not a constant – it varies by situation. A respected CEO may have no idea how to get through to his teenage son. A professional speaker might struggle with small groups. (I'm like that – really confident speaking with hundreds, and in conversations one to one, but interacting with 5 or 6 people at a time leaves me drained.)

Feeling uncomfortable in unfamiliar situations (which is where many conversations take place) is a natural response. Remember that others are probably uncomfortable too.

When you feel nervous, aim to modify your posture, gestures, and voice so they are similar to how you speak when you *are* confident. You will appear more sure of yourself, and others will be more at ease around you.

To gain confidence in your ability to make people listen, be willing to practice and grow your skills. Have conversations.

Take chances, to speak up, to meet new people in new situations. It doesn't matter if you do it *right* – just keep improving.

Grow comfortable interacting with strangers by making an effort to speak with people you meet casually – a store clerk, the football fan sitting next to you at the game, people at the gym or spa. Grow confidence professionally by voicing your opinions, ideas, and insights to colleagues and managers.

The more successes you have with something, the easier it seems. If you need to pretend confidence for a while until you get it, that's okay. If you need to borrow a coach's confidence for a while as you build your own, that's what they are here for.

Related tips: Getting started, Courage, Authenticity

Congruence

Congruence occurs when a person's words, body language, and non-verbal communication all send the same message. They match each other.

Learn to notice incongruence – mixed messages. You may notice that a staff member who two minutes ago said he was excited to hear about your new project is now slowly inching his chair closer to the door. Normally, you would not consciously notice the chair movement, but you might suspect or *feel* that he isn't really all that interested. Partly that's because your body picks up signals much more effectively than you can consciously process them. When you are watching for incongruence, you practice noticing the actual signals that give you that feeling.

If a client tells me that he is sure about ABC, but shakes his head as he does so, it's not congruent. When I inquire, he knows exactly what was said, but has no idea that he was shaking his head as he spoke. Once the conflicting message is pointed out to him, he can begin to deal with the internal issues and external manifestations, catch himself in the act, and the habit begins to change.

Be on the alert for your own congruence, as well. It will show in the words you choose, as well as in body movements, voice tone, and other non-verbal signals. When your inner frame of mind is solid and focused, your movements, voice, and language will automatically match, and ring true to others.

However, when you are not certain about what you are saying, your non-verbal signals will conflict with your words. People won't know whether to believe you, and may stop listening even while nodding their heads in agreement.

Last year, when my husband was very ill, I continued to go to networking events to meet new people and connect with colleagues, but truthfully my heart wasn't in it. Other people knew immediately that something about me was off, and I couldn't attract new clients or associates for the life of me. I might just as well have stayed home, where my heart was.

Related tips: Awareness, Observation, Non-verbal cues, Gestures, Emotion

Connection

Be willing to invest time getting to know and follow up with people you want great business or personal interactions with. Your personal connections matter as much as, or more than, your expertise.

During conversation, pick up clues about what is of interest or importance to others. Find something you relate to or agree with in what they say, and speak about that. Once people have a personal connection with you, they are more likely to follow your lead in other areas.

How you follow up and maintain relationships matters. When I called a former client to hear how she was, she uttered in complete surprise: "Oh, you care enough about me to call!"

I was surprised, too. We had been in regular contact by email, and had met for catch-ups many times. I thought I was doing well staying connected. I hadn't realized that it was a *phone call* from me was important to her. Now that I know what matters to her, it matters to me.

Surprise your clients, colleagues and friends with a random phone call, a personal note, or an article you cut from a magazine that relates to their hobbies or business. Stay close to those you have the privilege to know.

We all need connection as we stumble towards our dreams.

Related tip: Commonality, People matter, Interactions

Consciousness

Wake up. Pay attention to what you are paying attention to. Notice when you are in a trance (engaged with your own thoughts rather than the conversation) and snap out of it. The more you practice this, the more effectively you will learn to control both yourself and the conversation. If you are not alert, your automatic habits can take over without your noticing.

Everyone can learn to deliberately and consciously focus their thoughts on the task, person, or conversation at hand.

If you want to be listened to, you need to stay awake, aware, and focused throughout the conversation, whether you are speaking or listening. If you know a story so well that you could deliver it in your sleep, be extra careful when telling it. You could be sedating both yourself and the listener!

Related tips: Showing up, Control, Awareness, Observation, Energy

Content

Adjust the content of what you say to allow for the preferences of the other person. How do you know their preferences? By paying attention and listening. If a couple has been telling you about their vacation in specific facts and details, then when you present your business proposal use specific hard data, facts and details that they can study.

If a different couple tells you all about the people they saw and how it felt to be with their family on vacation, you can be more intimate and softer, and bring in how good your proposal will be for the team or people involved. Encourage them to see the big picture.

Customize the content of your presentation to the audience. If the audience is mixed, be sure to give both the hard facts and the more philosophical overview.

Related tips: Commonality, Listening, Connection, Observation

Control

If you feel powerless in conversation, stop that! Unless you live in a totalitarian state or you are speaking with your prison warden, there is no one else, nor any situation, in control of how you conduct yourself in conversation. You control everything you say, and how you say it.

Self-control is not repression, it is self-expression with restraint.

You control when, where, how, and if you have a conversation, who you speak to, who you listen to, and what you talk about. If there's something about a conversation you don't like, it's up to you to speak up and change it. No one else can do it for you.

There's no need to get aggressive about it, but you do need to be assertive. You need to know internally that what you say matters, and stand up for yourself. Do not allow anyone else's judgment or opinion to determine what you say.

Stay in control of yourself and be prepared to take control of your interactions in conversation if they are going off track.

Related tips: Inflection, Interrupting, Assertiveness, Emotion

Counting

In ordinary daily conversation, mentally count how many sentences you speak before you ask an open question that allows others to contribute. That will help you know if you speak more than necessary. If you have a tendency to speak for too long, people's attention will drift off anyway, so feel free to cut yourself short before they do.

Conversations are not formal presentations that allow you to speak at length to a captive audience. They are typically brief. Monitor what and how much you say. Don't say more than what others can process, usually five to seven sentences. Check this out for yourself: Do you ever lose track of what you were saying, or use the word *anyway* to bring yourself back on track? Those are indications that you've been speaking too long.

Did you just say 20 or 30 sentences in a row? Yikes! You would do better to speak in paragraphs rather than essays. Did you just reply to an open question with a one-sentence answer? C'mon, you have more to contribute than that.

There is no magic number of sentences that will keep people engaged. Simply speak briefly, pause to breathe, and if someone else wants to contribute, they will. If they don't wish to speak, go right on ahead and continue. You could have a knack for telling interesting anecdotes or expressing ideas that everyone wants to hear, so there is no need to cut yourself short. Do watch for audience signals and listening signals that tell you when to proceed or stop, though.

PS: Length of sentences matters. If you use *and, because, or then* ten times in one sentence, that counts as ten sentences.

Related tips: Brevity, Audience signals, Respect

Courage

You may not be at ease interacting with people you do not know well. If so, you have plenty of company. No one is completely comfortable interacting with strangers. Humans are unpredictable – we have no way of knowing in advance what others might do. Some of us find that fact of life exciting, others find it worrisome.

When you feel anxious or uncomfortable in situations such as business networking or social events, ignore any tendency you may have to automatically move towards the food table or the wall. Greet the people you know first, share a few comments, and then move along to meet others.

It may feel easier or safer to engage in conversation with people who already know you or your business, but it doesn't allow you to meet the people you want to meet – those who could become good clients or colleagues or referral sources.

And please don't stand around the side of a group, waiting for others to invite you into conversation. They won't. They can't read your mind, so you must take action and speak up in order to be heard.

There is no easier way to get what you want than to take courage and take action.

Related tip: Assertiveness, Control, People matter, Emotion

Credibility

People listen to trusted authorities. You may have the best skills in your field, but if you don't know how to appear credible, believable and trustworthy, both publicly and one-to-one, people won't pay attention to you, let alone do what you suggest. Your words, tone, and mannerisms must convey that you know exactly what you are doing.

Even if you are new in an industry, speak yourself as a trusted authority – an expert in what you do know. This is not about arrogance or bragging, it's about simply stating what you can do. If you have a degree or certification, related or not, put it on our business card. You earned it.

You have also gained skills and capabilities from your past experience. List them on paper for yourself. Pay attention to the ones that directly contribute to your trustworthiness in your current position. Do this so *you* know what makes you credible, and can speak calmly when you feel challenged by your lack of experience. Below is what I used to say eight years ago, before I had experience or testimonials. It always worked for me because I knew it was utterly true.

I spent 25 years teaching junior high school (people groan when they hear that). I loved it. I got to work with young people at the edge of their futures. That's where I learned to be able to see the brilliance of each human being, no matter what BS they pulled, and challenge them to let go of their excuses and get moving forward. That's what qualifies me to great coach. Only now I get to work with small business leaders at the edge of their futures.

Here's the key: If you believe in yourself and your own credibly, your voice, intonation, and mannerisms will convey credibility in every conversation. Some people will want you to have degrees or XYZ training, but on the whole, we trust others who have *been there*, and are successful at what we need from them.

Related tips: Credibility killers, Inflection, Authenticity, Non-verbal cues

Credibility killers

Certain words destroy credibility – subtly or suddenly. They signal a lack of confidence. Five words to notice and eliminate if you want your listeners to take you seriously are:

But – Indicates disagreement with whatever came before. If you use *but* repeatedly, you continually contradict yourself. And *Yeah, but...* responses challenge what others have said.

Should – Often used to bully others or yourself, as in *You should/shouldn't...* Besides, people rarely do what they *should*. They do what they want to do and commit to doing.

Try – Yoda said it best: "Do or don't do, there is no try." When you say you'll try to do something, others know you probably won't. A clear *Yes* or *No* is more honest and assertive.

Maybe – You can see that this is *kinda sorta perhaps possibly* like *try*. It's weak, inconclusive, and lacks conviction.

Guess – Guess? You *guess*? How can people trust someone who is guessing? State the facts as you mean them, and be willing to own your opinions.

Some mannerisms kill credibility and hinder listening too:

Nodding incessantly – Once in a while is great. Repeatedly nodding encourages the speaker to keep talking. Don't you want to be heard too? Nodding implies agreement but doesn't say it directly. Do nod when saying *Yes,* though.

Apologizing – for yourself, your opinions, your bluntness, your strengths or weaknesses, your forgetfulness, your interruptions, the other person's feelings! Unless you have made a mistake, don't apologize. Simply state the facts.

Smiling constantly – If you're happy, go ahead and smile. Break out in laughter if you want. However, if you wear a phony smile to keep people from knowing what you really think, it's annoying and we can see right through it. Be authentic.

Justification and rationalization – if you have to justify your point with long explanations and a dozen reasons why people should believe you, they won't.

Related tips: Authenticity, What you say matters, Respect

Definition of terms

Many arguments and misunderstandings occur because people fail to realize that they need to agree on what specific words or instructions mean (to both the speaker and the listener).

As much as possible, be sure that you and your listeners agree on what specific terms mean.

An example: John's supervisor pokes his head into John's office and says, "Hey, John, the water cooler is dripping." John looks up briefly from his desk and says, "Okay." What does that *okay* mean to the boss? That John will make sure it gets fixed? What does *okay* mean to John? That he heard the boss?

The next day, the drip continues, and the boss accuses John of not listening!

Different individuals even have different definitions of the word *listen*. Parents make statements like: "Listen to me!" when they really mean, "Obey me!" A wife accuses her husband of not listening, but the husband knows he has been looking at her and his ears are open, so what's the problem?

People often confuse listening with hearing. Hearing is what your ears do – input sounds – and listening takes deliberate attention. People think that when people are listening they must be understanding, which is not necessarily true.

Pay attention to how listeners respond to your words. If you see signs of confusion or disagreement, stop talking and ask them about it. This happened to me recently. A friend winced when I told her: "People lie." The meaning she attributed to the word *lie* was very different from the one I was using in that context. Once we agreed that a lie was not necessarily a deliberate untruth, but could be a misrepresentation, exaggeration, omission, wishful thinking, or even saying *Yes* when meaning *No*, the conversation flowed smoothly again.

Related tips: Language, Credibility killers, Understanding, Audience signals

Electronics

Electronic communication is both a blessing and a curse in the conversation world. It allows quick access to people and information, but unfortunately eliminates many audience and speaker signals that convey meaning. Texting and email tend to keep interactions at a surface level. An audience listens, understands and remembers best when information is simultaneously received through several senses.

We make our best choices about ideas, people and opportunities in much the same way as we make good buying decisions about products like electronics, clothes, or groceries. Whenever possible, we study them carefully, using as many of our senses as possible. We look at them, listen to them, touch them, smell them, maybe even taste them.

Would you be willing to marry someone you met online but had never smelled, touched, or tasted? Whenever possible, instead of a text or email, use phone or teleconferencing; instead of a phone call, meet in person or connect via video to ensure more effective listening and understanding.

Do not let an electronic device run, or ruin, your conversations. Answering a text or phone call during a face-to-face meeting tells everyone around that what you are doing is less important than what the caller may want. It also tells them that *they* are less important than whatever might come up with a beep. Ouch. Don't even look to see who is calling. Let them leave a message for you to check at your next break.

However, there are a few exceptions. If you must take a call during a meeting, tell the other person upfront that a call may come through that you must take, and explain just enough so they understand that it is critical.

One of my coaches always left his phone on the table if we were meeting in the late afternoon, so his 12 year old daughter could let him know she was safely home from school. I get that. I understand that. I admire that. I will gladly come second to a child's safety.

Related tips: Non-verbal cues, Tone, Voice quality

Emotion

Your emotional state affects, and sometimes infects, the emotions of people around you. People *pick up* emotions from each other. Remember a time when you were feeling upbeat until you ran into the doom and gloom mood of an angry colleague? Or a time you were walking in the mall and a stranger walked by in such a smiling good mood that you smiled right back?

Listeners will mirror your emotion when you speak. So if you want to get them excited about an opportunity, energize yourself first, and let it show. Then add vivid mental imagery to capture their hearts and imagination and get them excited too.

Control your own emotions in conversation. If you are bored, the listener will be bored, if you are unsure, the listener will be unsure, and if you are passionate, others will *catch* the passion from you. If your voice or manner is about as exciting as a slug, even the most determined listener will tire quickly.

Emotions can be useful tools, as long as you keep them within your control. If you have a strong emotional reaction to something, there is no need for a dramatic response. Breathe. Say nothing until you can think calmly. Remember that whatever other people say is about *them*, not about you. Do not take it personally. Hold any emotional overreactions in check – they are not what you want people to listen to, or remember you for!

Related tips: Control, Energy, Rapport, Respect, Non-verbal cues

Energy

The amount and quality of your energy impacts everyone around you. What kind of energy do you bring to conversation? Examine how your presence changes conversations. Are you adding or draining liveliness, making people nervous or comfortable, irritating or calming, causing confusion or clarity? If you can't determine the kind of energy you bring, ask someone you trust to tell you how they feel being around you. You need to know, so you can adjust your attitude to ensure you get the results you seek.

In one of my training courses, there was a young man who was so nervous and overeager that whenever he opened his mouth, everyone visibly cringed. His anxious energy, plus the innate empathy of others in the class, caused them to be nervous for him, and with him. The atmosphere was decidedly awkward every time he spoke. With feedback and courageous practice, he learned to relax more when speaking. Consistency in controling his energy and nervousness, however, will take further attention and practice.

Related tips: Emotion, Enjoyment, Control, Non-verbal cues

Enjoyment

If you can't enjoy yourself in a conversation, your listeners won't enjoy you either. When relaxed and comfortable, people think, speak, and listen more effectively. So make it easy for everyone – relax and enjoy yourself. Your listeners will be more open and receptive to you, and you will be at ease.

Do you have a good sense of humour? Then go ahead and use it. Your uniquely funny and creative self is probably quite appealing. Don't be afraid to behave a little out of the ordinary to gain or hold an audience, as long as it is playful, kind, appropriate, and safe to do so. Just be sure not to offend, and stop kidding around when others would prefer to move to serious matters.

Most conversations can be enjoyed, since few are life-changing or world-destroying. Suppress the impulse to analyze, theorize, and philosophize, and learn to enjoy the ride!

Related tips: Voice quality, Attitude, Audience signals, Energy, Authenticity

Enthusiasm

Dare to be enthusiastic. Listeners love dynamic, lively speakers who infuse them with energy. Placid, passive, unresponsive or emotionless speakers cannot hold their audience for long. If you bore people once, they won't listen so well next time. Bore them repeatedly, and you have taught them to dread conversations with you, and that is not what you want.

When your pace is too slow or your voice inflection monotonous, you force the listener to interrupt or entertain herself in her own mind.

I can't forget the time I heard a droning sound coming from a hotel conference room. I glanced through an open door, curious. What did I see? The audience was melting – their bodies were slumped in chairs, and several of them needed their forearms to keep their heads aloft. From the doorway, I couldn't tell if their eyes were open or closed. A projected white image covered with words held center stage, and the speaker (who seemed just as tired and bored – in fact his voice was the droning sound I had heard) was reading the words aloud. Torture! I was tempted to pop my head in and yell, "Escape! Quick while he isn't looking!"

When you have an opportunity to hear me speak, if ever you begin to get bored, do us all a favour, would you? Come up to the podium and wave this page in my face. (Oops, that won't work – I rarely stay in one place, you'll have to chase me around the room.) That'll wake us all up! And I'll buy your dinner later in gratitude.

Add, zip, energy, pizazz and passion to your voice, manner and message. Enthusiasm is infectious and magnetically attractive.

Related tip: Attitude, Enjoyment, Flexibility, Interest, Physical presence

Environment

Professional speakers are trained to check all aspects of the room before their presentation. You, too, need to know how the dynamics of the environment could affect how well people can see and hear you, and therefore how your words are received.

It's hard to have a positive impact on others if there is a disgusting smell coming from the kitchen, and no one listens well when they are shivering or boiling.

From the moment you pass through the doorway of a room, carefully study everything around you. Use all five senses. What is the size and temperature of the room? How is it set up? How bright or dull is the lighting? How many people are present, and how are they interacting? What is the noise level? What could distract you or others?

Do whatever you can to ensure the environment is conducive to effective conversation.

Related tip: Observation, Respect, Groupings

Every conversation counts

There is no day off from conversation, not even a half-hour lunch break. You are always speaking and listening. Whether you are in conversation with others, yourself, the dog, the TV set, or the driver who just cut you off in traffic, conversations are everywhere all the time. Stop now and listen to your thoughts. That's a conversation. Does it move you forward or stop you in your tracks?

Have you ever woken from a conversation you were having in a dream? Even while sleeping, we engage in conversation! Since thoughts don't stop, conversations are occurring everywhere, every time. And every one of those conversation impacts our thinking, behaviour and results.

What we tell ourselves matters. The tone of voice we use with a child matters. What we allow into our minds from the news or TV, how we feel about specific events, how we move, work, play – it all matters. Being alive is one big conversation! You and I are in conversation right now, although separated by time and space.

The power to create change is alive in every conversation. So pay attention, and make sure each conversation is taking you where you want to go.

Related tips: Accountability, Authenticity, Listening

Exit strategies

No conversation can, or should, go on forever. Each must come to an end. Many simply wind down and the ending is natural, effortless. Sometimes, however, you will want to exit a conversation before it is complete. How do you do that?

There is never a logical reason to boorishly leave a conversation, but there are many reasons to leave respectfully. You don't have to stay until the end.

If what you are hearing from someone is inappropriate, offensive, or no longer of interest to you, you have the right to change the subject or politely exit. Do not stand there passively or leave without saying anything. State your boundaries clearly. For example: *I prefer not to speak about others when they are not present. Let's talk about....*

Sometimes a speaker is simply talking too long, and a non-verbal signal will let him know that enough is enough. If the speaker is looking at you, neutralize your facial expression. Show no emotion. End eye contact. Look up or away. Eliminate all listening signals: the hmms, smiles, nods, leaning in, and head tilting that signal interest. Stiffen your posture and tighten your lips ever so slightly. If that doesn't work, turn your entire body, including your head, slightly away.

If non-verbal signals don't work, make a direct statement: *Excuse me, there's someone I need to talk to.* Or *Excuse me, I have a lot of work on my desk....*

Whatever you do, don't lie to get out of a conversation. Lying diminishes you in your own eyes, even if others couldn't know that the report isn't really due tomorrow morning, or the babysitter doesn't have a 9:00 pm curfew. Tell the truth as appropriate, or simply excuse yourself.

Related tip: Interrupting, Boundaries, Audience signals

Eye contact

Making appropriate eye contact is necessary to create good listening. It is difficult to build trust if you do not make eye contact effectively. In this culture, we assume low eye contact means evasiveness and intense eye contact indicates intimidation. Making adequate eye contact when speaking tells the listener you are sure about what you are saying.

Different cultures are accustomed to differing amounts of eye contact, so be sensitive to that, as well. As a general guideline in Western cultures, make eye contact about two thirds of the time when speaking, more when listening.

To make effective eye contact one to one, meet the person's eyes directly and focus mostly on their left eye. (I have no idea why that works so well, but it does.) Initially, match the amount of eye contact the other person makes, so they can feel comfortable with you, then increase or decrease to a level comfortable to you both. As trust builds, eye contact becomes natural and effortless.

Even though you may be able to listen or speak well without making much eye contact, it is a gesture of respect and confidence to look at the person you are conversing with. When speaking to a group, be sure to make regular eye contact with all members of your audience.

Related tips: Physical presence, Gestures, Rapport

Feedback

How can you tell if you understand the situation and are communicating successfully? In the long run, you will know because you get the *Yes!* you want. As well, every conversation is a continuous feedback loop. If you turn up your radar and observation skills, the conversation itself will give you immediate information about whether you are on track or off track.

The key is to frequently check for audience response, and then modify your approach until you get what you want. You already know how to do this! Remember a time you made a baby smile?

If you smiled at Baby and she didn't smile back, you didn't try the same approach repeatedly. Nor did you call yourself a failure, or blame her for not paying attention to you. You didn't give up. No. You tried a multitude of approaches until something worked: maybe you grinned ear to ear, made gurgling noises, added a lilt to your voice, made raspberries with your lips, or played peek-a-boo. You did whatever it took to make her smile. And when you wanted her to smile again, you repeated the strategy that worked.

Dealing with adults is similar. If they don't give you the response you want, notice it quickly and do something different. Much like airplane pilots regularly check their instruments to ensure the plane stays on course to arrive at its destination, great communicators frequently check and make minor adjustments to their communication to get the results they want.

Are you getting the responses you want? If not, adjust your course slightly. You do not want to be one of those people who don't pay attention to what they are doing or the effect they are creating, wondering why they lost a friend or sale or opportunity or concession.

Related tips: Audience signals, Flexibility, Intention

Flexibility

People are dynamic and complex. There is never a guarantee that they will listen, since what they pay attention to is their choice, not yours. Nevertheless, you can certainly influence them. That's why we speak – to influence, inform, persuade or convince. To have our viewpoints, experiences, and our contributions considered and accepted.

Although you cannot control other people, you can control your own approach. If you don't like the results you are getting, the only way to change them is to change your own behaviour. Do something different. Make adjustments to your non-verbal and verbal communication, and continue adjusting your approach until you get the results you want.

For example, if you want your colleagues to absorb the information you are giving, and it is evident their minds are drifting even as they stare at you, an immediate shift in your delivery style is called for. The key is to be flexible. If one shift doesn't do the trick, try out others. You could emphasize main points with more volume, ask for questions, call a brief break, enliven your voice, speak more quickly or slowly, create visual interest by using a diagram or demo, speak more directly, or visibly change your physical posture.

If you are at the front of the room, stand up really straight, shoulders back, take a deep breath, and move physically across the room.

Don't give up if the first technique you try doesn't work. Flex until you see a visible shift in the audience that signals they have re-engaged.

Related tips: Audience signals, Feedback, Observation, Voice quality, Physical presence.

Flow

Conversations are dynamic, constantly changing reflections of who we are and how we relate with others. Some conversations roar past all obstacles, others meander slowly to conclusion. Some circle back on themselves in endless loops, others forge ahead bravely.

Each conversation has a different flow. Is the kind of conversation you prefer wide and inclusive, narrowly focused, or somewhere in between?

Notice your participation in the conversations you join or instigate. How would you characterize your contribution?

If a conversation races off in a direction you don't appreciate, or leaves you behind, what can you do? Listen for a space, a pause or a topic shift, into which to add your contribution or question. Then jump in. Next time, practice adding your own momentum and style to the mix from the beginning. Don't wait for the conversation to go astray (or stagnate) before you contribute.

Since most people would rather be in conversation with a great listener than a great speaker, a good rule of thumb is to listen more than you speak. Those who are great listeners, as well as interesting speakers, will often be sought out for further conversation.

Related tips: Content, Energy, Counting, Listening

Focus

Are you able to focus on the conversation and the people at hand? If not, you'll want to develop your ability to eliminate sensory distractions and mental chatter. When your attention wanders, as it inevitably will, notice quickly and refocus on what is being communicated.

What about the people you are speaking to? Are they able to focus on the conversation? When I coach by phone, I request that clients turn off the computer, shut the door for privacy, and give the call their complete attention.

I saw a cartoon recently that defined multitasking as *messing up several tasks at the same time*. So true. An interrupted mind is much less effective.

Our brains cannot fully concentrate on more than one thing at a time, so if distractions are an issue, there is no point continuing a conversation. Find a better time or place.

A five minute focused conversation can accomplish more than an hour-long meeting disturbed by distractions and interruptions.

Related tips: Environment, Observation, Showing up, Exit strategies

Force

Although you can't ever *make* people listen, you can certainly help them pay attention to your point of view. Aggression is unnecessary and hurtful. Don't raise your voice, hold intense eye contact, grab an arm, block the exit, spew out a lengthy commentary, or in any other way attempt to get or hold attention by physical, mental or emotional force.

You have no right to impose your physical or mental power on others. People either give you their attention freely or it's worthless to you, anyway.

You might not know when you're being too forceful, because people often pretend to listen (a habit of Canadians especially), but internally they may be fuming, planning escape, or arguing with everything you say.

Pay attention to monitoring the volume and emotional tone of your words, as well as your physical posture. If you are seen as too aggressive, your reputation will suffer the consequences – bad news spreads quickly, and you will definitely be bad news.

PS: Being open, honest and direct is not bullying or overly forceful. It is assertiveness. However, if you are stating your opinion as *fact*, that's bullying (and a form of lying). Claim your opinions as your own.

Related tips: Respect, Voice quality, Hostage-taking, Gestures, Connection, Assertiveness

Fresh eyes and ears

Treat each situation as a fresh start. Do not let your past experiences affect (or infect) the opportunities in the present. Look and listen afresh. You are not the person you were last week (you hadn't read this book, for one thing), and neither is anyone else. You can't begin to guess what they have been through since this morning!

As soon as you think you already know what someone is thinking, or how the situation will unfold, your mind closes and opportunities vanish. If you think that someone won't listen to you today because he didn't listen last week. You're contaminating your mind (and therefore your results) with faulty assumption. Keep an open mind.

It's a new day and a new start. If you aren't sure that you have the skills to make others listen, then think: *I don't know, I think I'll find out*, and get out there and practice these tips. See what happens.

We do not know anyone (not even ourselves) as well as we might assume. Each interaction is new. The less you assume, compare or interpret, the more you can hear and speak the truth. Truth attracts listening.

Related tips: Judgment, Attitude, People matter, Observation

Gestures

If any of your facial or body gestures are not in alignment with your words, people will believe what they see, rather than what they hear. Ensure that you are as convincing in your gestures as you are with your words. Gestures that are too bold will push people away, and those that are too meek lack energy to pull an audience's attention.

Avoid gestures that convey weakness or lack of certainty: fussing with your hair or clothing, flapping your hands, playing with an object in your hands, nervous giggling, fidgeting, smiling constantly, nodding often, shrugging, toeing in, looking at the floor, shaking your head while saying something affirmative, covering your private parts or your butt with your hands.

There are hundreds of credibility-destroying gestures. To identify your own, videotape yourself and have a good hard look for gestures that are limp, indefinite or defensive.

Some gestures can make you seem aggressive or underhanded: Intense eye contact, wide stances, long strides, large arm or hand movements, stiff posture, tapping the table or your crossed arms impatiently, finger wagging, pointing, standing too close, both hands gesturing in front of your body, hidden hands, or wearing a *game* face. (You know this one. It's the face that football players adopt at scrimmage – intense and hard.) Avoid any large rapid movements; they will automatically be perceived as aggressive.

Where can you put your hands when speaking? Imagine you are at a cocktail party with a drink in one hand. That's a non-aggressive but confident position. Your other hand will naturally move with your words, and your gestures will fall close to your body between shoulder and elbow.

Related tips: Eye contact, Physical presence, Congruence, Non-verbal cues

Getting started

How can people listen to you if you haven't said anything?

Take the lead in casual social or social-business conversations. Most people are at least slightly uncomfortable in such situations and will appreciate your initiative. Introduce yourself, make a comment, or ask a question about the event: "Wow, it sure is noisy in here!" followed by a question, to get conversation started. Open questions, those which cannot be answered with a simple *Yes* or *No*, work best: "How's the food?", "What do you think of this venue?"

When I entered my favorite coffee shop last week, I saw a woman waiting in line who looked, from the back, just like a colleague of mine. I had an overpowering urge to surprise her with a hug from behind. However, caution won out, and I didn't. When she turned her head, I realized the face belonged to a stranger. I laughed at myself and told her how close I had come to hugging her.

Was she offended? No. In fact, she said she would have welcomed a hug. We had a great conversation while our orders were being filled, and my only regret is that I was too chicken to actually reach out and hug her. (As I write this, I marvel at the unique and friendly openness of Calgarians. I've never reached out my arms to a friend or colleague and not received a hug in return. I understand the blessed uniqueness of that.)

As you become more confident that you can start

conversations with anyone, even those very different from you in style and interests, it becomes easier to initiate conversations when the stakes are high. Even if you are quietly reticent by nature, I encourage you to welcome unplanned, casual conversations. They can engender more career and personal connections than formal introductions or elevator speeches.

Related tips: Introductions, Confidence, Connection, Flow, Courage

Groupings

At social or networking events, join groups of one or three if possible. (Every gathering is a networking event, even standing in line at the grocery store.) Two people chatting face-to-face could be deep into a conversation, and your joining them may be awkward or intrusive. Larger groups are easier to join, but it can be difficult to make yourself heard when several people are competing for the attention of the group.

One person standing alone is often eager for conversation, and when three people are talking, one of them usually will turn to you when you approach. Since groupings change often at networking and social events, you will have plenty of opportunity to meet and interact with new people.

Related tips: Observation, Boundaries, Getting started

Heart

People who have not fully listened to themselves will find it hard to listen to you. And if you are not paying attention to yourself and to the call of your heart, that may be diminishing your power in conversation.

The other day I met with a brilliant business strategist who was tired of corporate life but unsure choosing a new direction. She was looking for her *passion*. She had been researching different workable business opportunities, but couldn't decide. When I asked her what her *heart* wanted, she dropped her eyes and dug into her purse for a tissue. As she daintily dabbed at the tears, she replied, "I don't know."

What I suggested is the exercise I suggest to anyone struggling for focus, heart, contribution, belonging, or change. I suggested she take an hour each day to sit in stillness and listen to her own thoughts and feelings – just listen, maybe write. For one week. After some initial disbelief, she agreed. We'll see what happens for her.

Personally, I need that hour for myself every day. My mind is too active to inflict upon anyone without censure, so I sit and listen to myself each morning, watching my thoughts go by. It helps me align my day with my priorities and dreams – the places where my mind and heart agree. Sometimes an insight will cause me to write. In the eight years since I began this habit, stillness has proven itself a most valuable tool.

You can't show up fully – body, mind, heart and spirit – for another human being if you can't show up for yourself. And if you don't fully show up for others, they won't listen to you. (No matter how many techniques or strategies you know.)

Related tips: Showing up, Connection, Every conversation counts

Hostage-taking

If you keep talking at length, or speak loudly and aggressively, your listeners may feel like they are being held hostage to your story. They don't want to rudely leave until you are finished, but since you don't stop talking and they can't get a word in edgewise, they feel trapped. Is that your intent? I doubt it. You probably just don't know that you are engaging in an act of indirect aggression – holding the audience hostage to your words.

How long does it take you to finish what you want to say? Monitor yourself. Do you feel driven to finish your story or justification – no matter that the audience is no longer interested in listening? (A lot of lengthy talk is either storytelling or justification of opinion/action.) If you catch yourself talking when listening has stopped, what can you do? Simple. Stop talking immediately.

Then graciously apologize for monopolizing the conversation. "Oh my, I am sorry for going on so long about that. Please, let's get back to where we were...." then listen for a while. Reconnect with your audience, and allow the conversation to flow onward.

The next time you speak, you'll be careful to keep it brief so others are free to contribute as well.

Related tips: Counting, Brevity, Audience signals, Force

Impressions

Consciously choose the impression you want to portray. Business-wise, you can't go wrong with a professional demeanour in dress, speech, and behaviour. Yes, be yourself, but be a version of yourself that others can easily respect.

How you dress matters. I attend many events at the Chamber of Commerce. Many of my local coaching clients are business owners. At one of the networking meetings, participants show up in a wide variety of attire – from dark suits to painters' coveralls, according to their profession. For other events at the same location, we all dress to the nines and shine our shoes. You need to know what will be the norm. Although you do want to distinguish yourself in a crowd, don't do it by under-dressing. Better to slightly overdress.

You wouldn't expect to find a scruffy sweaty fellow in a plaid shirt, and worn overalls sitting in the CEO's office with his muddy booted feet on the desk. Nor would you expect to see a perfectly groomed and accessorized woman in a skirted navy suit and high heels daintily picking rocks in a farmer's field. Dress for the role you wish to play.

Hygiene matters, too. Are your body and breath clean and odor-free? Have you maintained your teeth, styled your hair neatly, dressed in well-fitting clothes, shined your shoes, or applied appropriate cosmetics? Is there some lettuce stuck between your teeth? Be sure to check the mirror (and your breath) before you enter situations where an audience will be subjected to your personal hygiene habits.

PS: A sloppily tied tie can be worse than none at all, as it will distract attention from what you say, and transmits an unspoken message of carelessness.

PPS: Avoid strongly perfumed products. Most of us are highly sensitive to smell, and prefer fresh-washed human to flowers or spice.

Related tips: Inhibiting, Energy, Rapport

Inflection

If you wish to be credible and trusted, do not speak in questions. Make statements. If a sentence isn't a question, and you do not expect an answer, do not raise the tone or pitch of your voice at the end. (Read the last three sentences aloud. Your voice tone will vary up and down as you read. That's good. But does your voice rise at the end of sentences? If so, you are speaking in questions and killing your credibility. Stop that!)

If a new acquaintance tentatively offers, "I'm a mortgage broker?" it is very different from firmly stating, "I'm a mortgage broker." She may be well qualified to get you a spectacular mortgage rate, but the questioning inflection conveys uncertainty, which discounts her skills and instills doubt in the listener. (At least she doesn't say, "Right?" after every few sentences, which is even more destructive to credibility.)

Listen for inflection patterns when you speak. Are you, too, speaking statements as if they were questions? For credibility and confidence sake, ensure your voice inflection falls slightly at the end of each sentence. (Not too much, or it could sound like you are issuing orders!)

When inflection rises, credibility drops.

Related tips: Voice quality, Tone, Emotion, Credibility

Influencers

When networking for business or career advancement, seek out the influencers in the room. Influencers are people with personal and/or social power. Others approach them for advice, referrals, and mentoring. Influencers have a wide network of contacts and information, and of all the people in the room, they know best how to connect you with people you want to meet.

How do you recognize influencers? Well, first by asking the people you already know: "Who would it be good for me to meet here today?" And secondly, by looking and listening – who is it that you and others are automatically drawn to? Although powerful people don't look much different from anyone else, they do tend to be noticeably humble, positive, and engaging. Influencers seem to be magnetically attractive, but the secret isn't magnetism – it's assuredness, optimism and energy.

Influencers are people you will want to establish ongoing relationships with. You will benefit, and chances are that you have knowledge, expertise and referrals to offer them as well.

Related tips: Who's who, People, Introductions

Inhibiting

You have the ability to inhibit your own unnecessary or inappropriate thoughts, habits, gestures, words, and tones of voice. Some conversation topics, as well as gossip and criticism are never appropriate.

Many years ago a mentor taught me three quick questions to ask myself before I speak. They have always worked for me, except when I forget to use them. When you are not sure what might be appropriate to say, think before you speak. Ask yourself these three questions:

Is it true?

Is it kind?

Is it necessary?

If any of the answers is *No*, do not say what you were thinking of saying. Squelch it, bite your tongue, or take a time out, whatever you have to do to stop yourself from speaking. Then speak only what is true, kind and necessary – with tone, gestures, and words that match your intention.

Related tip: Intention, Congruence, Force, Heart, Every conversation counts

Intention

Know your reasons for being in any conversation. What specific results do you want to achieve, and what do you want others to think, do or say?

Do you want to meet new people, make friendly chitchat, support a colleague, challenge a decision, evaluate options, give feedback, set a plan, gain compliance, convince, prompt action, brainstorm ideas, build trust, establish yourself as an expert, give information, arrange a further meeting, create laughter, meet industry leaders, support a colleague, create change, tell a story, or...?

Prepare yourself mentally to listen and speak according to how you wish others to respond to you. If you want to be seen as a nice guy, or a great story teller, or a kind soul, or an intellectual or a master of your industry, you will behave differently, speak and respond differently, than if you want to persuade others to follow your lead.

There are many different reasons to be in conversation. You need to know *your* reasons. If you don't consciously make that decision, someone else will make it for you, and you could find yourself at the mercy of a complainer who wants to convince you how bad things are. Is that what you want? No? Then you must know exactly what you *do* want, and why.

Related tips: Control, Consciousness, Every conversation counts

Interactions

Notice the interactions around you. Where is laughter (if any) occurring? Where are more serious discussions being held? Who is holding others' attention and who is standing or sitting alone? Are people keeping to themselves or gathering in pairs or in groups?

What is the temperature of the conversation around you? Is it icy, cool, lukewarm or fiery? I don't recommend joining a group of individuals who are standing stiffly apart from each other and conversing crisply, even if you know them well. Better to join the warm animated group that is chatting easily, even if your manner is usually quiet or cool.

What kind of interactions do you prefer? If you are an enthusiastic go-getter who wants to be heard in a room full of casual chatter and laughter, you need only be yourself. In a solemn environment, however, take a gentler, quieter, more serious approach, at least initially.

If you prefer a calm one-to-one conversation, look for someone standing alone. If she makes eye contact or smiles as you approach, she will likely enjoy a conversation. I meet the most wonderful people that way.

Remember to also pay attention to the effect you have on others. Ensure that your contribution to the interaction leaves people feeling better than before you joined them.

Related tips: Awareness, Emotion, Rapport, Groupings

Interest

One of my coaches was fond of saying, "If you want to be interesting, be interested." Pay attention to what matters to your audience. It is easier to capture their attention when you speak about what is important to them. Their minds are already open to it.

Then deliver your message in ways that are interesting. Many people don't know why or how to listen effectively and it's not up you to teach them. Your responsibility is to make them *want* to listen and to keep their ears willingly on your message. However, since humans can listen three times faster than normal speaking speed, every listener's attention will wander from time to time. If what you are saying is of interest to them, they will quickly refocus on what you are saying. Speak clearly, calmly and concisely to prevent too much mind wandering.

Dare to be downright enthusiastic and passionate about what you are saying. Even if the information you have is of utmost importance to listeners, you will lose them if your personal presentation style is dry, monotonous, boring, or lengthy.

Related tips: Enthusiasm, Emotion, Tone, Voice quality

Interrupters

Allow for the fact that people process information at varying rates. Someone who is eager and enthusiastic may interrupt you when you are talking. Don't be too rough on those listeners who become so engaged in what you have said that they add their comments before you are completely finished speaking. Their eagerness to contribute could be an indication that they are completely connected with your idea or suggestion, and that's a good sign!

However, if someone interrupts you at an inappropriate time or with a change of subject, and you need another minute to finish an idea, this is what you can do: Hold one hand at chest level, palm toward them in a gentle stopping motion, and say, "Could you hold that thought for a moment, please." (It's a statement, not a question.) Finish what you had been saying, and then be sure you ask them for their comment. "Did you have something you wanted to add?"

Related tips: Boundaries, Timing, Assertiveness

Interrupting

Stop the air space hog. You don't *have* to listen to anyone, or stay in any conversation. In fact, you may be doing a disservice to those who talk a lot when you allow them to rattle on and on. If they continue the habit, they could destroy both their credibility and their likeability. So go ahead and interrupt!

It is appropriate and respectful to interrupt kindly but firmly. Interruptions that occur while the speaker is breathing between sentences, and that are related to what was just said, are not usually seen as offensive. Listen for something you have in common with the speaker, agree with what he says, and then redirect the conversation toward where you would like it to go.

Contrary to popular female belief, the world won't end if you interrupt.

Related tips: Boundaries, Beliefs, Force

Introductions matter

Except for very formal occasions, you need not wait to be formally introduced. It's generally acceptable (at least here in the casual West) to introduce yourself to people. This sends a message of personal confidence and caring. It also puts you in control of the conversation from the start.

Even if you are anxious about meeting new people at business events, make a point of extending your hand and saying, "Hello, I'm ....". The other person will automatically tell you their name, and then you can ask them an open-ended question about their job/business. That takes the pressure off you, and as the other person talks you will gain valuable information about who they are and what you have in common.

When I facilitate for corporations, I am usually quite nervous at first. However, I deliberately introduce myself to several individuals as the participants settle in, learn their names, and chat with them. I want to experience them as individuals rather than as strangers. It is much easier to present to people I know than to a group of strangers. My talk then becomes simply an extension of that first interaction – a conversation with the people in the audience.

Related tips: Commonality, Connection, Every conversation counts

Judgment

What assumptions, judgments, and interpretations are you allowing to colour your interactions with yourself and your prospective listeners? When you evaluate situations, are you making those assessments based on fact or opinion?

Judgment occurs when we add an emotional charge or an interpretation to what is essentially a neutral event. (And all events are neutral – we add our own meanings, feelings, and preferences to them). Any negative judgment or assumption you hold about yourself or others interferes with your effectiveness in ensuring your message is heard and understood.

To get better results from your interpersonal interactions, become aware of how your opinions, preconceptions, prejudices and judgments about people, places, events, or yourself interfere with your ability to speak clearly, openly and directly.

Deliberately set any judgment, assumptions, and interpretations aside, and focus on the realities of the present situation and the people you are with. Your communication will be cleaner, clearer, and more welcome.

Related tips: Observation, Fresh eyes and ears, Beliefs, Emotions

Kenny Rogers knows

When you have done all you can to communicate well, practiced every A – W tip in this book, and you still cannot get someone to listen, stop trying so hard! Some battles are not worth fighting. Take a breather and relax. Acknowledge that you have done the best you can to influence the person or the situation, and surrender to reality – you cannot control others.

Kenny Rogers' lyrics are just as appropriate for conversations as for poker games: *"You gotta know when to hold 'em, know when to fold 'em, know when to walk away, and know when to run...."*

Related tip: Exit strategies, Respect, People pleasing

Language

Each person has their own *personal language*: unique vocabulary, phrasing, sentence structure, and vocal patterns. The use of language also varies across cultures, companies, generations, families, and situations.

Why bother learning to speak someone else's language? So others don't have to struggle to understand you, so you can influence, connect, and be understood when you speak to them. Using your listener's language shows that you are just like them, and we tend to like people who are like us. We listen to people we can relate to.

Pay attention to the language patterns of an individual or group. Then match some of their specific words, similar length of sentences, and voice quality. You've probably done this many times before without realizing it, just as great communicators do. You speak more formally around business associates, using specific industry vocabulary, longer sentences, and formal tone. You speak more casually, excitedly, and openly when having a great time with friends.

What I'm suggesting is that you do that a bit more deliberately. Matching language to the situation strengthens connection. If someone says she's *mad*, respond by asking her what is making her mad, not what is making her *livid*, *annoyed*, or *furious*.

Groups often have words and phrases that distinguish them, and if you want to fit in, match their words, even if it means jotting notes and then memorizing a whole page of acronyms when you join a new corporation. That's exactly what one of my students did when she started with a new oil and gas company.

Related tips: Rapport, Observation, Listening, Connection, Style, Pitch, Pace and Projection

Listening

The cry of every human heart is to be heard. The best thing you can do for your business and personal life is to become known as a great listener. Listening creates space for people to be comfortable just as they are. And listening is a great disarmer – people will tell you things you couldn't ever have discovered by talking. Feelings, ideas, and issues come spilling out into the listening space.

Begin listening and studying people consciously as you interact. They'll reveal their needs, preferences, dislikes, styles, priorities, motivation, commitment, and satisfaction criteria. You can't learn all that while you are talking. You need to listen.

Listen to what is actually being said, rather than to what you would like it to be. Not active listening, but *accurate* listening. As a listener, your job is not to judge or evaluate, agree or disagree, interrupt or hurry the other person along. Just listen.

You could be an expert in your industry, but if you miss the clues that people leave, your message or responses could land far from the mark and you might not know what on earth happened.

Consciously pay attention to listening fully and carefully. As you listen, ask yourself: *What are they saying about how they think and how they feel? How do they see the world? What makes them distinct from other people I know? What can I learn from them? What do we have in common? How can I assist this person? How can we benefit each other? How can I adapt what I say in order to connect more fully?*

Related tips: Language, People matter, Awareness, Observation, Rapport

Manners

Your mother was right about the importance of good manners. When you join a group already in conversation, asking *May I join you?* lets them know that you want to be a contributing member of the conversation, and demonstrates that you are considerate of their feelings as well. Few people could refuse such a request. Once you have joined the group, be sure to exhibit good listening skills to determine the context of conversation before you contribute your own ideas.

And... your mother was right about the importance of always saying *Please* and *Thank you,* too.

Please use appropriate and polite language that does not offend any type of person or group. Although catty or rude comments may seem funny in some situations, they are never completely appropriate, and rudeness sends a message to everyone listening that the speaker holds himself to pretty low standards.

When you want to move away from a group that you are no longer directly talking with, say *Excuse me* quietly, incline your head across the room as if there is someone calling you *over there* and move away gracefully. Powerful communicators do not hang around groups they are not directly involved with.

If your conversation with a single person is winding down, offer to introduce him to someone else. Once they begin chatting, excuse yourself as above.

Related tips: Exit strategies, People matter, Listening

Non-verbal cues

You can't *not* communicate. Everything you say without words also impacts conversation. Non-verbal signals are quickly picked up by the unconscious mind, which interprets, evaluates, and decides instantly whether you can be trusted, or if a *fight or flight* response is needed.

Fair? Maybe not. Nevertheless, your posture, stance, head tilt, shoulder set, eye contact, facial expression, gestures, physical closeness, and body movements – even what you are wearing – impact how your words will be received.

Everything others see and hear tells them who you are and whether they should listen to you. Even how you walk – whether you stride, drag your feet, shuffle, or teeter on heels – sends a wordless message.

Pay attention to the subtle messages your body and voice is sending. Communication isn't just about words.

Related tips: Voice quality, Physical presence, Gestures, Observation, Credibility killers, Pace, Pitch and Projection

Observation

If you are paying more attention to your inner thoughts and feelings than to the realities of your circumstances around you, what you *don't* notice will hurt you.

To get the coaching edge in conversation (which allows you to access the best outcome from the current opportunity), consciously choose to remain alert and pay attention to exactly what is happening around you, even as you speak.

Studying your environment and the people in it takes discipline, patience, and focus, but the knowledge can help you distinguish exactly how best to have your message heard.

To gather data accurately, first suspend preconceived ideas, personal biases, and opinions. Put them on hold for a while. That will free your mind to examine the situation from a position of *neutral observer*. Observing neutrally means carefully studying people and situations as if you were a scientist studying a foreign community. Assume nothing. Gather sense data only: sights, sounds, feelings (physical), smells, and tastes. Pay attention to *what is*, rather than what you would like it to be.

The more you know about the situation and each person in it, the more precisely you will be able to target your message to the specific situation and audience. You will eventually become aware of even slight shifts in your audience, rather like telling identical twins apart – there are all sorts of little cues if you look closely enough.

Observation sure beats guessing about what people are thinking or feeling, and saves you the bother of rattling off stories that are irrelevant to your listener's experience.

Related tips: Awareness, Audience signals, Environment, Television practice #1, #2, #3

Pace, Pitch, and Projection

The pace of your speech affects the listener. If you speak too slowly, others may be unable to quiet their minds enough to concentrate on listening. If you speak ultra quickly, the listener will miss much of your message. So don't try to cram in lots of information by speaking quickly. Choose what is most important to convey, then speak at a reasonable, slightly fast pace. Vary your pace to add interest and vitality.

When you are excited or frightened, unconsciously the muscles around your voice box tighten, causing a higher pitch. Normally, women's voices are pitched higher than men's. If you usually speak in a voice pitched too high though, that indicates a lack of emotional poise. If your voice is low-pitched, vary your pitch when possible – by allowing it to rise with excitement, for example.

Projection is the strength of your voice, and the distance that your voice carries. If you are speaking to one person, ensure that you are loud enough to be heard easily. If you need to project your voice across a room, aim to reach the person farthest away, breathing from the belly to ensure you are heard loudly and clearly. A well-projected voice demands respect and attention.

Related tips: Inflection, Breathing, Voice quality, Control

Patience

Don't give up on people – on yourself or anyone else.

If speaking up or being listened to is difficult for you, be patient with yourself. It takes time to establish new habits. Give yourself lots of room to learn, stretch and practice – just as you gave yourself lots of chances to learn to walk.

Be patient with others, too. Understand that some personality types need to tell a story before they can make their point. You can't change them, and if you want to get closer to them, both patience and compassion will be needed.

If you are the one who is telling the story before making the point, keep practicing the tips here, especially *Structure*, and understand that although people are trying to listen, it can be very difficult for them to wait for you to get to the point.

Related tips: Brevity, Structure, Courage, People matter

Pauses

Before you speak, pause. This gives you time to think and gather your thoughts, and indicates to the previous speaker that you have considered what he was saying. If your words follow too quickly after others have spoken, especially if you begin with *Yes, but...* you will come across as inconsiderate, overeager, immature, or self-centered, which you probably aren't.

Remember to pause while speaking, too. Effective speakers and conversationalists use pauses for effect. They pause after important points to allow them to sink into the listener's mind.

Air is good for you!

Related tips: Voice quality, Emotion, Control, Breathing

People matter

That's the real reason I am writing this book – because people matter. Their well-being matters, their flourishing matters. If people don't matter to you, give this book to someone else – someone who can care about others.

When I first started my coaching business, I asked my coach how to prioritize so many tasks. He said something that has become my credo: *People first*.

Those of us who are privileged to have conversations that matter with people who care are a blessed lot. Every person matters. Every voice matters. Each one of us is unique, precious, and irreplaceable.

People deserve to be treated as if they were the most valuable beings on earth, because they are – including you, me, and the homeless guy pushing his cart down the street. It's important that people listen to you, and that you listen to them.

Related tip: Patience, Respect, Attitude, Judgment

People pleasing

You can't please everybody with what you say or how you say it. It's hard enough just pleasing yourself! Sure, pay attention to people's responses, respect and consider them, but do not give up your best interests for what you are guessing others might like or want. The world doesn't need your self-sacrifice.

You can learn to influence most people to your point of view. That's all. You can't hurt or heal their feelings or make them angry, since they are in complete charge of what they think and feel. You can, of course, be considerate and kind as you share your opinion, story, or information.

And you don't have to climb every mountain. You and your potential client, for example, may have such vastly different thinking and communication styles that no amount of adjusting how you deliver your message creates rapport and understanding. If that occurs, or if you do not have the specific services or products he needs, stop wasting your time and his. It is appropriate to refer such a client to someone else. This may be necessary even after you have been working with him for some time, freeing you both up to interact with someone with whom you can create better results.

Related tips: Control, Inhibiting, People matter

People watching

If you want to be the person who gets others to listen, you need to know how a variety of people behave and relate. Here's a practice: when you are in public locations like shopping malls, restaurants or bookstores, pay attention to the people around you. You will notice a vast diversity of humanity readily available for study. How much can you learn about people by simply watching them, studying how they move and talk? Lots! Try it.

It isn't necessary (or advisable) to stare though – you can access a great deal of information with your peripheral vision, or a casual glance. What are people doing? How do they interact with each other? Which people are really listening to one another and which are simply going through the motions? Is that silent couple comfortable with each other or are they seething inside? How do you know that, exactly? What other specific clues can you pick up by simply watching?

By practicing your people-watching in casual situations, you develop more precise attention skills to help you *read* a variety of people during your conversations with them.

Related tips: Television practice #1, #2, #3, Awareness, Observation

Perfection

Perfection is completely and utterly unnecessary and undesirable in human beings! Perfection is for androids, plastic dolls, and cups of tea. Constantly driving hard for perfection will make you seem nervous and aloof. Stop trying so darned hard – your anxiety makes the rest of us nervous.

We imperfect people don't want to be around perfect people, either. They make us regular folks look bad. We listen better to regular people, and even irregular ones!

Years ago, while I was still wondering if I wanted to coach professionally, I spent an hour with an established coach. He was wearing a perfectly tailored suit and tie, and spoke smoothly, sentences flowing from his lips so precisely that I was mesmerized. He was so perfect that I stared. But the problem was that I couldn't relate to him, so I didn't hire him, even though he had been saying all the *right* things.

I didn't want to be around perfection. I needed a coach I could be honest with, someone who could put up with my frankness and my millions of questions. Someone I could tell the truth to, someone who would see through my excuses, be blunt with me, push me to achieve, and encourage me to coach in my own way. So I hired a bald coach with big ears and goofy grin who spoke frankly and challenged me to be myself and play full out.

Related tips: Authenticity, Style, Vulnerability

Personal growth

If someone had a conversation with you last month, he doesn't want to have the exact same conversation with you again this month.

Make sure that you are learning and growing, both personally and professionally, so that you have fresh and interesting tidbits to add to your interactions with others.

Stay up to date on current political, regional and local events, charities, sports, technical and business news. Delve into hobbies, expand your musical repertoire, read fiction and non-fiction, or take some classes.

Keep growing in knowledge and understanding of yourself, your business, and your community. Learning new concepts and exploring innovative ideas will maintain you as a vital, lively personality who always has fresh material, ideas, and experiences to share.

Related tips: Interest, Commonality, Content, WIIFM

Physical Presence

Adopt a strong physical presence. Walk, sit and stand like you mean business! To have your ideas taken seriously, stand tall, feet solidly planted. Bring your shoulders down and back, chest out, chin up and level, head centered, eyes steady, face composed. Relax and breathe normally.

Never diminish your value by slouching or staring at your hands, crossing your legs when standing, taking itty-bitty steps, or by staying at the periphery of a group. You have a right to be there, to take up physical space and air space, as much as any other person.

Don't take this too far, though. Avoid holding your body rigidly or woodenly. (Bodies are built to flex and move.) An ultra-stiff body posture is downright scary and pushes people away. You may be the most attractive person on earth, but if you stand like Frankenstein and it's not Halloween, people will still want to get away ASAP.

If your posture was a statement, what would it say?

Related tips: Presence, Impressions, Breathing, Credibility, Congruence

Preparation

Prepare appropriately for every meeting, whether you arranged it or someone else did. What is the meeting for? Who will be there and why? Who will be in charge? What will your role be? What is the agenda? What will you need to be able to say or do? How formally or informally will people be dressed? Is there parking? (Worrying about whether you parked in a legal spot, or having to run four blocks in the rain can destroy your calm cool ability to hold powerful conversations.)

If you do not prepare ahead, you could be caught off guard, and the words that escape your mouth may be words you reproach yourself for later. Learn as much as possible about an event beforehand so you can be in an appropriate mental state when you get there. Don't try to prepare perfectly, however. You don't want to make yourself anxious, and no one can prepare for everything!

Related tips: Perfection, Emotions, Time, Impressions

Priorities

When you know what matters most to people (their priorities), you have an advantage in conversation with them. Speaking directly into their priorities is the most efficient way to get them to listen to you, and agree with you.

This tip is especially helpful in sales, and in any situation requiring that you persuade others to accept your point of view. How can you find out what people really prioritize, what truly matters to them? By asking a simple question: *What's important about that?*

Several years ago I sat down with a young financial planner. A third of the way through her presentation, I asked her how she chose that particular company. (I'd heard the same script and contrived questions from others before her, and, frankly, I was bored hearing it again.) She said she was good with money, and wanted to help families. I asked her: "What's important about that?" She said that she knew many young families were struggling, and that her company provided financial education for them.

I asked her what was important about that. She reported that she had immigrated to Canada a few years ago, and had struggled to figure out the Canadian financial system.

I said, "Wow, it must be wonderful knowing that you can help others avoid the kind of struggle you went through." Her face lit up in recognition of what mattered most to her – saving others from the kind of financial struggles she had endured.

Still somewhat in awe of her own heart for the business, she listened intently as I spoke about how coaching could help her make a significant difference in even more lives.

Why did she give me her attention? Not because I am some kind of charismatic guru, but because I had asked what was important to her, had uncovered her deeper priorities, and helped her claim them. Easy. No *sales* pitch needed.

That young woman became a highly successful financial advisor with a unique and memorable presentation. I know. It was a privilege to coach with her.

Related tips: Authenticity, Vulnerability, Intention, Commonality

Problems

Problems and pain connect people. When our lives or businesses or personal lives are working well, we don't need to talk about them as much. But when we have a problem or issue, we seek out other perspectives, and we listen to other viewpoints. Being able to offer a fresh point of view on a problem is the mark of a great *coach* and conversationalist – someone others will listen to.

Human beings thrive on having problems to solve, challenges to meet – that's how we grow. If we didn't have that innate drive, we would never have learned to walk. What now seems to us simple – walking – required our immense determination when we started, but we managed, because it is in our nature to grow, learn, and rise above our limitations.

Problems bring us together. So go ahead and talk about problems you had or are having. People will listen. Then spend most of your time asking others about, and helping them solve, their problems or issues. They'll respect you for it.

Related tips: Brevity, Rapport, Stories, Commonality, Vulnerability

Rapport

Developing rapport is about getting on the same wavelength as the person you are talking to. Rapport works to create trust and confidence because we relate most easily to people who are similar to us, and automatically unconsciously respond positively.

We naturally develop levels of rapport with others. You can see deep rapport among friends when they unconsciously mirror each other's language, gestures, and posture.

It is also possible to *deliberately* build greater rapport by matching the person's body language, speaking speed, voice quality, eye contact, or breathing rhythm. When you match your approach to someone else's, you make it easier for him to feel comfortable with you. Matching and mirroring send the message *I'm just like you.*

How do you know you've built good rapport? After matching the other person for a while, subtly shift your body posture and see if they follow. If they begin matching your posture, you will know you have established good rapport and you can lead from there.

Related tips: Eye contact, Breathing, Emotions, Priorities, Language, Connection

Respect

People who are in conversation with you are giving you their precious time, energy and attention. And you are giving them yours.

Respect those irreplaceable gifts, and ensure that both of you have opportunities to voice your ideas, and to develop relationship and/or business.

The best relationships and businesses are built on a solid foundation of mutual respect and appreciation. Do not confuse respect with likeability or tolerance. Respect is much more. It is holding each other in high regard for expertise, skills, achievements, talents, characteristics, qualities, actions, or ethics.

Do you speak to be liked, or to respect and be respected?

Related tips: Acceptance, Connection, People matter

Results

Know exactly what you want to achieve from a conversation. Then, after the conversation, measure your communication effectiveness by results. Simply measure – there's no value in judging, blaming, or shaming yourself if you didn't get everything you wanted. No one gets exactly what they want all of the time, or even most of the time. We just come as close as possible, celebrate successes, and try again.

Did people listen to you? Did you present yourself professionally, speak clearly, and articulate well? Did you get the outcome you wanted? What specific approach, words, or behaviour worked to make people listen to you? What detracted from your effectiveness? Did you stay on track with your intentions during the conversation, or get sidetracked by someone's fishing story?

If your intention was to get three people to make appointments with you to discuss how working together can enrich business and speed results (that's often my usual networking intent) how many meetings did you set up? What could you do differently next time? What learning from past successes (your own or others') could you draw upon?

Related tips: Intention, Attitude, WIIFM

Showing Up

Make sure you show up on time and with your attention intact. Some people's bodies arrive at an event long before their minds do! It's as if they sent their bodies on ahead to save them a seat, but their attention and focus are far behind. Sometimes they even start conversations without being fully present.

Make sure you aren't one of those people. Be ready to give others your full attention and focus, whether as a listener or a speaker.

Settle down, eliminate mental chatter, and breathe. Feel your feet on the floor, and deliberately take a few deep breaths. Show up in body, mind, heart and spirit, so you can give the conversation your complete attention for the entire time you are in it.

Related tips: Courage, Confidence, Focus, Awareness

Silence

Have you ever noticed an older couple in a restaurant, so completely comfortable with themselves and each other that they do not need to talk? They enjoy the food, smile at each other now and again, maybe comment a bit on the quality of the fish, but most of the time they are silent. That's communication too – a very peaceful, gentle variety.

You don't have to talk to communicate well, to be understood, or to understand. Your world won't collapse if a conversation hits an impasse or grinds to a halt, and you can't think of what to say next.

Of course, the harder you struggle to figure out what to say, the more words will elude you. So relax into the silence instead. Someone, maybe you, will move the conversation forward in a moment or two.

Related tips: Emotions matter, Awareness, Vulnerability, Attitude

Stop! Look! Listen!

Remember when you were a little tyke and someone taught you to *Stop, Look and Listen* before you crossed the street? That was really useful advice for keeping you safe while allowing you some freedom to explore. And it's still a valid technique for paying close attention to the dynamics of conversations. Don't go rushing forward without paying conscious attention to the *traffic*, or you could very well get run over, or (perhaps worse) completely ignored.

When you arrive at any event location, assess the situation thoroughly. Environmental, hierarchal, social and emotional factors exert a strong influence on interpersonal interactions, including receptivity to your ideas. Before you approach anyone or say anything, remember to *Stop, Look and Listen* first.

Knowing exactly what is occurring for the people around you will help you distinguish what type of communication is most appropriate for the situation.

Related tips: Observation, Awareness, People watching, Listening

Stories

Great storytellers don't have to make people listen – they captivate the audience with words, gestures and voice, turning communication into an art form.

Let me be really blunt here. You may indeed tell lots of stories, and you may have practiced some of them repeatedly, but that doesn't make you a great storyteller. Many people think that since they tell long stories and no one tells them to shut up, they must be good storytellers. Not so. It may only mean that the listeners are extremely polite.

When you want to enhance an idea or a concept, a story can be a wonderful tool, as long as it has a clear beginning, middle, and end. Relate your story with liveliness, brevity, and charm, and be sure to keep an eye on the audience for their responses.

Personally, I love listening to great stories. I just don't tell them very well. I don't have the flair for drama. I'm better at strategizing and provoking, not entertainment.

Related tips: Brevity, Emotion, Flow

Strengths

The most powerful tool for change and development is increasing self-knowledge. The more you know your strengths, the more you can develop them and make your weaknesses insignificant. What are your personal strengths in the conversation realm?

Pause your reading and list a few of your conversation strengths here:

Thank you. It took courage and commitment to write those down. Now here's the bad news: All strengths, even the ability to have people listen to you, begin to work against you if you overuse them. Like any of the tips in this book – if you overuse them, or use them rigidly, they become pitfalls rather than workable tools. Are your strengths working for you, or do you need to balance them so you are in control of when and where they will be best employed?

When you know that you tend to keep your opinions to yourself, are quite forceful, or are quiet and polite, you can use that knowledge to adjust your speaking to get the results you want.

If you tend to be very expressive, you need to be aware of when that is working for you and when you are overdoing it by becoming too intense, pushy or loud.

Patience, for example, is a valuable asset. However, when you are overly patient with others, you may never get a word in edgewise. And if you are too patient with yourself, you may not take the initiative to change some aspects of your communication style that are interfering with your ability to make people listen, speak up and be heard.

If you don't pay attention to your strengths and how you are using them, you could keep doing what you've always done, expecting different results.

Related tips: Patience, Inhibiting, Interrupting, Authenticity, Presence, Awareness

Structure

Deliberately decide what you are going to say, and structure it for ease of listening and understanding.

Speaking structure is a lot like paragraph structure. The first sentence should contain the main idea of what you are going to say. Then come a few supporting details. The details must be directly related to the main idea. Do not allow distracting ideas to jump into your paragraph. You may then end the paragraph with a summary statement related to the main idea. Just as a properly constructed paragraph helps the reader understand, a properly constructed *verbal paragraph* helps the listener understand.

Study the paragraph above. It is deliberately structured. Not everything you say or write has to be structured that formally, but please at least state the main idea first, so the listener has a context for the rest of your message. Otherwise you are pouring out your ideas or your wisdom without giving the listener a cup in which to catch them.

Tell them what you're going to tell them, then tell them, then tell them what you told them. It is that simple, whether you speak for a minute or an hour.

If your goal is to share an assortment of information, write a book of tips and strategies, then make sure the title gives the reader the context, or cup.

Related tips: Brevity, Counting, Preparation, Control, What you say matters

Style

Study communication styles. Each person prefers specific language structure, and uses distinctive non-verbal patterns. You will develop connection and rapport most effectively when you match the other person's communication style, at least initially.

You already have some experience doing this: You use different facial expression, mannerisms, expressiveness, tone, speed, vocabulary, sentence length, and volume when speaking to a toddler than when you are speaking to an expert in your industry. By honing your ability to match and mirror a few of other people's language patterns, you can gain almost anyone's interest. Why? Partly because they won't have to translate what you say in order to understand it, and also because we humans tend to automatically like and gravitate to those who are *just like us*.

Your own style matters, too. Make sure you know and recognize your own style, and that it is memorable to your audience. (*Bland* doesn't count as an appropriate conversation style and neither does *overbearing*.)

Related tips: Language, Impressions, Being memorable, Rapport

Television practice #1

Watching reality television is an easy, time-effective way to practice your observation skills without having to learn them on the spot in conversation. Here's how. For five minutes, study the setting of a reality-based show. Look and listen. Notice how the environment affects interpersonal interactions.

Secondly, study the participants for 5 minutes. Identify differences in their personal styles by watching and listening to exactly how each character moves and interacts.

Finally, choose one major character to be the subject of your focus for 10 minutes. Turn the sound off, and watch what he does. How does he silently show what he is thinking or feeling? What emotions are affecting him? What specific clues does he give that indicate whether or not he is listening?

Those non-verbal cues give you some data that will help you distinguish when others are listening to you. The wider the variety of characters you study, the better your perception of listening/non-listening styles becomes.

Related tips: Observation, Television practice #2 and #3, Non-verbal cues

Television practice #2

With the sound on, study one of the characters on a reality television show. Does he remind you of someone you know? What is that resemblance?

What style of communication does he respond to best? Does he keep his opinions to himself or verbalize them? When does he speak and when does he remain quiet? Does he speak more about emotion or tasks? Is he determined and resolute, or is he open to input from others? Which other characters does he listen to and which ones does he ignore? Does he respond to being encouraged, or being told what to do, or being challenged, or...?

What specific evidence can you find to support those answers?

Can you see that studying even one character can help you discern how people communicate and can be influenced in real life?

Related tips: Observation, Television practice #1 and #3

Television practice #3

Study your reactions to various TV characters. What is it exactly about a TV host's way of speaking that catches your interest or has you roll your eyes? What guests on talk shows do you automatically like or hate? What did people do or say specifically that causes you to react to them with affection or dislike?

Noticing your automatic reactions to others can help you pinpoint your own biases, preferences and soft spots. Any of these preconceptions can severely limit your ability to understand the very people you want to influence.

And any preconceptions will also influence how you speak and what you say in the moment – hampering your effectiveness in working with those people to whom you have an unconscious reaction.

Related tips: Observation, Judgment, Acceptance, Television practices #1 and #2

Time

Set clear time and topic boundaries for scheduled interactions. Agree on an agenda and stick to it. Others will soon recognize that your time is valuable, and that you value their time as well.

It could be a simple as: "Hi, Mary, for our meeting tomorrow, let's limit it to 15 minutes. I'd like to hear how the X project is coming along, fill you in on my progress, and figure out our next steps. Are you good with that?"

Ask people to listen for a specific length of time, and don't go over that time limit. It sounds like this: "Hi Mark. I would like to speak with you for five minutes about (whatever it is). Do you have the five minutes now, or would later this afternoon be better for you?"

Related tips: Boundaries, Assertiveness, Preparation

Timing

Time your arrival at events and meetings. The goal is to arrive when there are some people in the room, but not to be one of the last to arrive. You need time to assess the room and the people in it, and to network and to get to know people informally before any formal activity commences.

When you are scheduled to meet with someone, aim to arrive first, so you can settle in and feel comfortable. Late arrival shows disrespect, and you don't want to send that kind of message to your potential listeners and clients. Plan to arrive 10 minutes early, so that if you take a wrong turn or get cut off in traffic, you will still be on time.

The specific time of day a conversation or presentation takes place can make or break a deal. By late afternoon, people often have made so many decisions that their brains are tired. They are unlikely to be able to listen well enough to grasp all of what you offer. If at all possible, have important conversations in the morning.

There is an optimal time for everything. The best timing is often right now. Procrastination sucks – problems grow, and opportunities diminish.

Recently I asked a new client if he had been successful at a networking event we had just attended. Had three people committed to meet to discuss their finances? Had they agreed on timing? He said he had met some people, and he had their cards to call them later. What a waste – they had been listening to him at the meeting, but by tomorrow when he calls... who knows if or how they will respond?

Please, do not let any opportunity go by. Make a solid connection, or book a further meeting if that is your goal, while people are there with you, interested in you, listening to you.

Related tips: Assertiveness, Getting started, Interactions matter

Tone

If only people were as careful and particular about their tone of voice as they are about the ring tone on their cell phone!

You can tell when a friend is frustrated, a colleague is irritated, or a child is feeling powerless. Those emotions show in their tone of voice. Read this sentence aloud as indicated.

"I wanted that report by Friday."

Neutral

Angry

Disappointed

Excited

Whining

Sharp

Can you hear a distinct difference in the tone of your voice? So can your listeners. Are you being careful what emotions (or biases) are revealed by your tone of voice? Be careful to use tone of voice deliberately to add to your message. You can gain skill by practicing neutralizing your tone when you are feeling high emotion, and perking up your tone when feeling tired.

If you can't hear different tones in your own voice, it may be that you do not use much tonal variety when you speak.

Ask someone else to read the sentences so you can hear the tones, and make a conscious effort to use more variety of tones yourself.

How does your tone of voice normally sound? Confident, condescending, rushed, apologetic, friendly, capable, crisp, business-like, playful, or...?

Extra tip for parents: The moment you begin to feel frustrated, your children will know it. They are experts at discerning emotion by tone. If you allow your frustration to show, you have lost control of the conversation. Your kids will know that *they* have control, since obviously you have lost yours. Ensure that you can speak with cool, calm assuredness (no matter what). When you lose your cool, you lose.

P. S. Please be sure you are not speaking in a sleepy, sedating monotone. Unless you intend to hypnotize us, add some *variety* to your voice. Don't go overboard, though. Singsong voices are childlike. As a start, deliberately vary your tone, inflection, pace, or volume as you speak.

Related tips: Voice quality, Energy, Enthusiasm

Understanding

When you join a conversation, and before you speak, ensure that you understand what others are talking about. In order for your words to fall on receptive ears, your own comments must be relevant. Random statements that come out of the blue are confusing at best, and reputation-destroying at worst.

In casual conversations, ask questions to clarify any terms or concepts you haven't understood.

When you want to people to listen, it is your responsibility to ensure that they can understand what you are saying. This means being aware of, and deliberately using, appropriate content, language, vocabulary, and voice.

Pay attention to your listeners and adjust your communication until you get the response you want. Invite input or ask questions so you know that others understand exactly what you mean. If you don't check regularly for understanding and engagement, you are gambling with your results. And just like in Vegas, the odds are stacked against you.

Related tips: Definition of terms, Audience signals, Awareness, Content

Voice quality

Do you love the sound of your voice? If you don't, others may not either.

The way your voice sounds to you internally is not the same as others actually hear it. To hear your own voice clearly, record yourself speaking and listen to the playback. If the idea of listening to yourself makes you uncomfortable, have courage. As far as I know, no one has died from doing this exercise. It's no more dangerous that looking in a mirror.

Study the recording. What is the overall quality of the recorded voice: is it calm, rhythmic, scratchy, rough, tight, tentative, seductive, breathy, smooth, crisp, musical, discordant, soothing, restful, whispering, irritating, awkward, rambling, piercing, snappy, whiney, gentle, commanding, breathless, confident, measured, sluggish, uneasy, impatient, hasty, slow, fast? Identify five adjectives that describe your voice. You will probably discover that your voice is not nearly as bad as you thought it might be.

Then ask someone you trust (preferably someone with a good voice) to listen to the recording and describe your voice. Their honest feedback will help you distinguish exactly how to speak to have others listen more easily. We are automatically drawn to people with great voices, but good voices work just fine too!

Related tips: Observation, Enthusiasm, Judgment

Vulnerability

There is more power in vulnerability than in the illusion of invincibility. An immediate closeness arises between people when one speaks honestly about a personal shortcoming, or reveals a slipup that does not cast him in the best light. An error, a challenge, a mistake made and revealed will often draw others to you magnetically. The ability to express vulnerability shows that you trust people will not judge you, and people appreciate being trusted.

Remember that everyone around you, including you, has experienced or is experiencing a difficulty or pain of some sort. None of us is always strong and confident. If you give the impression that you don't need to learn any more, that you don't need any help, or that you have somehow already made it, you will push away the very people you are capable of assisting.

More than anything else people may want to know about you, they need to know you are human – just like them.

(Which doesn't mean you should walk around recounting endless mistakes to everyone who crosses your path, or burst into tears every time you see a puppy.)

Related tips: Authenticity, Connection, Commonality, Perfection

What you say matters

Words have power. They can hurt or heal, attract or repel, embrace or exclude, push people away or pull them to you. Choose your words with conscious attention.

Pause to think clearly in the moment, and consider your words carefully in accordance with the result you want. If you want someone to agree with your philosophy, you can speak more abstractly, in big pictures and big ideas that engage the imagination. If you want to show a company how their employees can save an hour a week by learning your Blackberry efficiency techniques, use very precise language, statistics, and hands-on demonstrations.

For clarity's sake, if you know a more specific word for what you want to say, and it doesn't sound odd coming from your lips, go ahead and use it. People understand many more words than they normally use. Be careful though – just because a word is long and seems impressive doesn't mean it's the right word for the circumstances.

It's a good idea to stay away from acronyms, slang, and technical language if there is a chance anyone will not understand. A new employee in one of my communication skills courses said that for months she couldn't understand what others were saying at company meetings, since they were using so many acronyms.

Remember that every word you say tells the listener who you are, what matters to you, what you are feeling, and how you think. Is what you are saying an accurate reflection of you?

When what you say is clear, calm and confident, and your words clarify, enlighten, inform, enliven, encourage and uplift, listeners will gather around you.

PS: For much of my youth I believed that if I could just say the right thing in the right way, then others would listen to me, hear my ideas, and maybe even agree with me. I spent a great deal of energy trying to figure out exactly *what* to say, and that was painful! I encourage you to take this tip gently. Pay attention to, but don't allow yourself to struggle with, words. Sometimes simply expressing yourself is more important than anything else.

Related tips: Content, Confidence, Language, Audience signals

Who's who

I am not suggesting that you go out of your way to speak with all the well-known or influential people at a business or social event, but do be sure to acknowledge the hosts of the gathering. Connect with them before the meeting starts, and thank them before you leave; perhaps send a note afterwards. The person who invited you will be able to introduce you if it is a formal gathering, and at casual events you can ask someone you know to point out the hosts.

Never underestimate the who's who at a casual meeting or event. Wealthy and influential people melt into a crowd, showing up in the same jeans with casual shirt and jacket as everyone else. Be willing to talk with everyone. You just never know when a connection will be made.

One last word about who's who: It doesn't really matter who is *publicly important*. Every person you meet is someone you can learn from. Get to know them for who they are first, and sure, speak about business casually – you never know who knows someone who is exactly the one you need to design your book cover or lead your team.

Personally, I love chatting with the courageous (but maybe a little hesitant) souls who show little or no trappings of success. I was actually deep in debt when I hired my first coach, and I know that over 90% of multi-millionaire entrepreneurs started out just that way!

Related tips: People matter, Manners, Connection, Every conversation counts

WIIFM

People who listen to you are giving you their two most precious resources: their attention and their time. They have their own reasons for listening. When you know what those reasons are, you can address their unspoken question: *What's in it for me?* (WIIFM)

Tell them early and specifically the *benefits* of listening to you, or using your services, or doing whatever it is you want them to do. For example: an electronics salesman says, "I have a way you can protect your investment in this product," before he says a word about warranties.

When you are introducing an idea, business, or service, remember to address the benefits (what people will be able to achieve with your product or service) early on, so they have a reason to keep listening, and later to remember the benefits of working with you.

Related tips: Listening, Connection, Intention, Being memorable

FROM THEORY TO ACTION

A mentor once told me that if he gets even one great idea from a book, speaker, seminar, or coach, it has been worth ten times the investment. I have found that to be true. And when I put an idea into action, it is worth ten times more than that!

I tell my clients never to leave a great idea or insight hanging in the air – make a commitment to take immediate action. Why? Because it's not true that knowledge is power. Knowledge cannot help you make people listen. Knowledge will not get your ideas accepted or your message understood. Knowledge is not power.

Applied knowledge is power... and wisdom.

So yes, think about the tips you have read here. Then decide and commit to using a few, and get out there and take action! Here's part of a *reflection* process that my colleagues and I use:

Ask yourself:

What insight, strategy, or learning have you gained?

What makes that idea valuable?

What does it tell you about what you could do or not do?

How can you adapt the idea to your situation?

How, where, and when could it work for you?

How could you improve on the idea?

What is the best time and place to start?

Then we begin experimenting, putting the insight or idea into action. It's all practice after that!

We've found that there is no need to analyze, theorize or philosophize. Simply reflect briefly, and then move into action.

Growing in powerful self-expression and making people listen requires that you do something different based on the ideas, tips and strategies you have read here.

What actions have you decided to take?

To take ownership of your intentions, write them here. Putting your commitments on paper strengthens them.

First three action items:

1.

2.

3.

To optimize the value you have received from this book, regularly review and use these tips as appropriate in your business and personal life. Reflect upon which ones will work best for you, and then use them. You will soon realize that others are indeed listening to you!

THAT'S A WRAP!

Just as I was putting the final touches on the tips, a colleague asked me to sum up the three most important things a person has to know about how to make people listen. Here's what I heard myself say:

You have to believe – in yourself, your message, and the value it brings others.

You have to speak clearly, briefly, and confidently (and it won't ever be 'perfect').

You have to focus on helping others, and set aside your own fears, especially the fear of what others might think.

I hope that what have read here will give you a good start at making people listen. Every day will bring you new opportunities to practice. The game of mastering self-expression never ends – it changes and grows, just like we do.

Now it's time for me to release this book into the world – to be embraced, criticized, loved, or ignored by people. That's the nature of all self-expression, all communication. We do the best we can at the time and hope for the best!

I hope you will listen: to yourself and to others. I hope you have learned something valuable and will take action that helps you be heard and understood. I hope above all that you remember that you, too, deserve to be listened to.

Thank you for *listening* to my message here. I look forward to hearing about the improved results that the tips produce in your life. Please be sure to tell me all about them.

I look forward to listening to you one day soon.

Remember that every voice matters. Your voice matters.

Jean

CONTACT INFORMATION

Your comments, ideas, results, applications, and celebrations are important to us. We'd love to connect with you.

Email: jean@listeningprofessor.com

For presentations or coaching based on *How to Make People Listen*: jean@execucoach.net

Listening articles, videos, and courses:
www.listeningprofessor.com

Coaching, coach training, and speaking:
www.execucoach.net
www.jeanhudson.ca

Follow Jean on Twitter: @listeningprof

Facebook: www.facebook.com/hudsonjean

Business profile and events:
http://ca.linkedin.com/in/hudsonjean

INDEX OF TIPS

E

F

G

H

I

J

K

L

M

N

O

P

R